Why Truth Matters

Why Truth Matters

Ophelia Benson and Jeremy Stangroom

continuum

Continuum
The Tower Building
11 York Road
London SE1 7NX
www.continuumbooks.com

15 East 26th Street
New York
NY 10010

British Library Cataloguing-in-Publication Data
A catalogue record for this book is available from the British Library.

ISBN: 0-8264-7608-2

Library of Congress Cataloguing-in-Publication Data
Benson, Ophelia.
    Why truth matters / Ophelia Benson and Jeremy Stangroom.
        p. cm.
    Includes bibliographical references (p.) and index.
    ISBN 0-8264-7608-2
    1. Truth. I. Stangroom, Jeremy. II. Title.

BD171.B44 2006
121–dc22   2005051783

Typeset by BookEns Ltd, Royston, Herts.
Printed and bound in Great Britain by
The Cromwell Press Ltd, Trowbridge, Wiltshire.

Contents

Acknowledgements

The authors would like to thank Julian Baggini, Sarah Douglas and the team at Continuum, Hywel Evans, Komal Gilani, and Cheryl O'Donoghue.

1 The Antinomies of Truth

It is not new or surprising or puzzling to think that we don't always love the truth. The truth is we often fear and hate it. There can be truths about our own health or that of people we love that we hate with a final ungainsayable loathing. There can be truths about our situation, whether financial or cosmic, that make us uneasy. Keats told us that Beauty is Truth, Truth Beauty, and that that is all we know on earth. Romantic poets had many virtues, but rigour of thought was not always one of them. It's hard to think of a less true generalization.

There are true facts about, for instance, how many people were murdered in horrible terrifying degrading circumstances in any one of history's many instances of massacres, war crimes and ethnic cleansings. It is unlikely that anyone knows the true facts, but there are true facts. Melos, Mycalessus, Carthage, Constantinople, Montségur, Armenia, Auschwitz, Lidice, Cambodia, My Lai, Srebrenica, Rwanda – for each placename there is an exact number; for each corpse there is a history. And there is nothing remotely beautiful about any of it. Nothing whatever.

It is no great wonder then that we do not always love and embrace the truth. We suspect that at least part of the truth (in some times and places, nearly the whole of it) is that we are a nasty, short, brutal species with a strong taste for torture and murder, that whenever there is an opening we make serious sustained energetic efforts to eliminate whole branches of our own kind, that even in peaceful times we persecute and coerce and extort labour from each other, that anything the smallest bit admirable, disinterested, ameliorative about us is only a thin surface element, a bit of gold leaf or paint a millimetre deep, while the greedy murderous savage goes all the way down, to solid bedrock.

This truth or suspected truth is all the more unbeautiful in light of our situation. 'Thrown' into the world, as the existentialists liked to put it, with only each other – more of the brutal murder-prone primates – to call on for help. 'History to the defeated / may say Alas, but cannot help or pardon', Auden remarked. History cannot, and neither can anything else. Not the *deus absconditus*,[1] not the stars, not the universe, not other animals, not plants or rocks, not numbers or ideas, not goodness or beauty or, even, truth.

This sort of truth may be a number of things – bracing, interesting – but it is not exactly beautiful, and it is certainly not comforting or reassuring. So it could be said that we have good reason to hate and fear the truth; to resist and reject it in order to take refuge in more emollient, cheering, hopeful interpretations. '[F]acts are precisely what there are not, only interpretations', Nietzsche said: so if one interpretation makes us feel lost in space, we might as well pick another. That is the thought.

Counter-arguments can seem feeble. It's all very well to say that optimistic replacements for the truth encourage us to let our guard down, to be incautious, to install too few safeguards against our sadistic and predatory tendencies; such arguments are not terribly powerful in the face of the desire to feel minimally cheerful about ourselves and each other, and our prospects, and our story.

Thus the upshot is we don't love the truth, not all of it, not all the time. We reserve the right, most of us, to accept some truths but to reject others, no matter how well warranted, how supported by evidence, how tightly argued. 'That's as may be', we say or think, smiling thinly, 'but there are other ways of viewing the matter.' No one is infallible, no one knows for certain, and I will think what I like. Jamie Whyte is familiar with the reservation:

It's just that, on some topics, many people are not really interested in believing the truth. They might prefer it if their opinion turns out to be true – that would be the icing on the cake – but truth is not too important … And to register this, to make it clear that truth is neither here nor there, they declare, 'I am entitled to my opinion.' Once you hear these words, you should realize that it is simple rudeness to persist with the matter. You may be interested in whether or not their opinion is true, but take the hint, they aren't.[2]

That's one way to deal with unwanted truth, and one of the simplest: the mental reservation; the internal denial. A one-step algorithm: just say no. But there are many others: authority, obfuscation, evasion, alternative evidence, taboo, asking unanswerable questions, distortion, shooting the messenger.

The mental reservation method is useful and popular because it is simple and therefore easy: a labour-saving device. It obviates the need to come up with alternatives, suggest other hypotheses, give reasons, offer evidence, think through implications. Another method that shares this labour-saving character is the appeal to Authority: external denial rather than internal.

This method was more viable in the past, in premodern times. It was never completely efficacious even then: there were always cracks, flaws, escape routes, places the authorities weren't monitoring closely, laws or warring barons that rendered central authority less than all-powerful. But for centuries, most literate people were clerics, universities were explicitly theological, and thought-crime could be punished with fire or sword. Magna Carta or no, Queen Elizabeth I had John Stubbs's right hand cut off because he wrote a pamphlet critical of her potential marriage with the Duc d'Alençon, and she was considered mild as monarchs go.

This role of Authority – to tell people what to believe and think, or at least what to appear to believe and think – can be seen in two ways, or from two directions. It was coercive and authoritarian, but it was also in a sense liberating: it liberated people from responsibility and the hard work of thinking. It was external, imposed, top-down, but that very imposed top-down externality made it a source of inner security and comfort. It's a familiar thought, even to defiant rebellious types (or perhaps especially to them) that it can be very restful just to give up and take orders – the despairing emptied-out rest of Winston at the end of *Nineteen Eighty-Four*, but rest all the same.

The social world has always lavishly provided this comfort, and still does for many. Holy books, tradition, fiats, laws, priests, judges, monarchs, inquisitions, prisons, chains, axes, fires, manacles, expulsions. The advantage of all these is the clarity, the lack of ambiguity (unless one notices the places where holy books contradict themselves, but people seem not to).

The system was never total. There were always isolated pockets that seemed to ignore it entirely, such as Montaillou (if Emmanuel Le Roy Ladurie's account of it is accurate), and there were always people who flouted it either openly (thus risking, and often getting, extreme punishment) or in secret. There were hedges and limits, even to strong monarchy, as Charles I discovered. The system became less total over time, as various upstarts came along to throw spanners into the works. The Renaissance, secular scholars, worldly popes, Copernicus, Machiavelli, Luther, Galileo, Montaigne, Bacon, Descartes, Newton, Bayle, Spinoza, revolutions and regicides – all did their bit.

Nevertheless, it may be that the basic idea – that the truth is what the higher authorities say it is, rather than what it is independent of any humans – had its effect on habits of thought over all those years. The notion that certain special humans can decide what truth is entails believing that human decision has some sort of transformative effect on reality, bestowing truth or withholding it; such a belief may foster other kinds of epistemic confusion. Thus for instance it is still a very popular thought that, whatever the truth may be, the important thing is that everyone should be on the same page; that social cohesion and peace are much more important for everyone's wellbeing and smooth functioning than are truth and free enquiry. On this view, truth is a political matter rather than an epistemic one. It is what it is good for the community to believe, not (necessarily) what corresponds to some state of affairs in the world or some mind-independent object. This system or method is still popular not only because it promotes unity but also perhaps because it frees up a lot of energy. Letting the higher authorities, whether autocrat or majority opinion, do our denying for us saves us large amounts of time and effort, allowing us to get on with other things – earning a living, having fun, improving the world, smelling the flowers. The thought 'Reverend X says that's wrong' or 'Our Leader says that's an Enemy-idea' can be a highly effective bypass or shunting device to deflect our muscle and brain power to work or reproduction.

Another tactic is to cordon off certain sets of ideas, to declare them special, inviolate, taboo, sacred: different from ordinary, mundane sets of ideas, as in Durkheim's distinction between the sacred and profane. Salman Rushdie (who has intimate experience with this distinction) talked about this cordoning off in an article at *Open Democracy*:[3]

> At Cambridge University I was taught a laudable method of argument: you never personalise, but you have absolutely no respect for people's opinions. You are never rude to the person, but you can be savagely rude about what the person thinks. That seems to me a crucial distinction: people must be protected from discrimination by virtue of their race, but you cannot ring-fence their ideas. The moment you say that any idea system is sacred, whether it's a religious belief system or a secular ideology, the moment you declare a set of ideas to be immune from criticism, satire, derision, or contempt, freedom of thought becomes impossible.[4]

This tactic has become a powerful way of shutting people up, because it operates not as external authority and coercion, which can be resented, resisted, laughed at, but as internalized guilt and bad conscience, which are much harder to resist or laugh off. If The Bosses tell us 'you may not think that', there seems to be a certain nobility in defiance and rebellion. It is the Lucifer/Satan move, the Prometheus move – which, as Shelley noticed two centuries ago, can be much the most appealing and self-respect-creating: 'Milton is of the devil's party without knowing it.' But when the taboo issues not just from The Bosses but also from The Community, especially from The Community speaking (at least apparently) on behalf of the victimized and downtrodden, then resistance becomes altogether more difficult and painful.

This is arguably one of the most powerful and effective tools of denial going at present. Simply invoke the holy name of The Community or Religious Beliefs or Their Culture, and very often disagreement will slam to a halt, in a fog of embarrassment and guilt.

There are at present many such ring-fenced, Taboo no-go areas in disputes over truth; places where disagreeing with people is treated as tantamount to peeing in their soup. Where people see themselves and are seen by others as entirely justified in puffing up like a pouter pigeon and declaring themselves Offended, which being interpreted means, not 'Let us eagerly continue this discussion in an attempt to discover the truth of the matter, without fear or favour', but rather, 'This discussion must immediately cease in order to spare my outraged feelings, and it would be no bad thing if you rescinded what you just said, apologized humbly, and made a large donation to a charity of my choice by way of recompense.'

Religion is the most obvious of these no-go areas. Declarations of offence have become all too familiar. A small group of (male) Sikhs forced the closure of the play *Behzti* by the (female) Sikh playwright Gurpreet Kaur Bhatti in January 2005. The incident was an interesting example of the Special, Taboo, ring-fence, Sacred idea at work, because the objections of a very small minority of Sikhs got respectful attention – more respectful, it seems fair to say, than profane secular non-special groups would have received. The Birmingham Rep met with self-appointed representatives of the offended Sikhs (and did not meet with other, non-offended Sikhs, no doubt because non-offended Sikhs, being unoffended, didn't put themselves forward) to discuss possible alterations to the play. The

Rep declined, in the event, to make all the changes these putative representatives asked for, though it did make some. There were protests, marches, and then a small riot which damaged the theatre, whereupon the Rep ended the run of the play. The playwright received death threats and went into hiding.

There was another – as it were matching – protest a month later, this time by vocal Christians, about the BBC broadcast of *Jerry Springer the Opera*. Again, a small but noisy and indignant group pitched a fit about being 'offended', and when their demands were not met, some protestors made death threats against BBC executives.

It is interesting to note that these forms of Taboo are about art, specifically fiction, not about scientific research, scholarship or enquiry. Being about fiction, they are in a sense not about truth at all. But in another sense they of course are about truth – about larger truths that the artists in question are – or are taken to be – pointing to through their fictions. That is why the protests are made. The protesters do not like the picture that is given of the Prophet, or the behaviour of some Sikhs, or Jesus. And it is the notion of offence, outrage, violation, of Taboo-tampering, that seems to inspire the violence of the protests (all three included death threats). That sense of outrage and violation is one branch of truth-denial.

An interesting aspect of the Taboo device and attitude (and it is both – device and attitude or habit of mind) is that it misses the real difficulty.[5] There can be a much more cogent objection to truth-claims: not that they offend, but that they do harm. Not the pseudo-harm of causing mental pain, of causing people to think thoughts that they don't like thinking, of causing perturbation and unease, but the real, material, physical harm of, for instance, discriminatory laws and customs and practices, and/or of hatred leading to violence, killing, ethnic cleansing, ethnic rape, war crimes. We will discuss this subject further in later chapters. The distinction between offence and harm is surely crucial, but it gets blurred and overlooked in much public discussion of these subjects.

We have looked at two popular techniques for denying unwanted ideas and truth-claims: what one might call the command approach – Authority says that's wrong – and the Taboo approach. There are others: evasion and concealment, Shoot the Messenger, obfuscation, changing the subject, distortion, asking unanswerable questions and rival evidence.

Evasion and concealment can take various forms, and can be individual and personal as well as public and institutional. One can conceal unwanted ideas from oneself via simple ignorance. One can read nothing, or read only that which one knows in advance will proffer no unwelcome thoughts (and the same applies of course to watching and listening). One can select all one's sources of input carefully such that an alien upsetting suggestion will simply never be heard or read. One can, in short, simply use a very large and very fine-meshed filter.

Shooting the Messenger is generally more difficult in modern times – although not always and everywhere difficult enough. Anaxagoras, the friend of Pericles, was prosecuted for impiety and left Athens as a result. Voltaire characterized the matter this way in the *Philosophical Dictionary*:

> Anaxagoras dared to maintain that the sun is not guided by Apollo riding in a quadriga; and he was called an atheist and obliged to flee … Aristotle was accused by a priest of atheism; and, not succeeding in having his accuser punished, retired to Chalcas. But what is most odious in the history of Greece is the death of Socrates …[6]

Giordano Bruno was burnt; Galileo was coerced. Books were placed on the papal index. John Wilkes and Leigh Hunt were imprisoned. Stalin and Hitler silenced people in wholesale lots, as did the Red Guards and the Khmer Rouge, Mao and Pol Pot, Pinochet and the Shah. Salman Rushdie was fatwa'd, a translator of his book was murdered, Naguib Mahfouz was stabbed, Theo van Gogh murdered, Ayaan Hirsi Ali threatened; and so on, into the bleak future.

Confusion and obfuscation are arguably the best way to go. Obfuscation is legal, it's easy, there is always an abundant supply and it often does the trick. The more unclear it is exactly what one is arguing, the more trouble one's opponents will have in refuting one's claims. They may well give up and wander off in fatigue and exasperation. It's always worth a try. (We will say more about this in Chapter 7.)

It's also arguable that obfuscation is what postmodernism is all about. Clouds of squid ink in the form of jargon, mathematical equations whose relevance is obscure, peacock displays of name-dropping, misappropriation and misapplication of scientific theories are often seen in postmodernist 'discourse'. Nietzsche, Heidegger, Heisenberg, Einstein, Gödel, Wittgenstein are hauled in and cited as saying things they didn't say – sometimes as saying exactly the opposite of what they said, as Rebecca Goldstein argues in *Incompleteness: The Proof and Paradox of Kurt Gödel*.

Among 'humanist' intellectuals who do invoke Gödel's name, he is often associated with the general assault on objectivity and rationality that gained such popularity in the last century. I'd often find myself pondering which would be the preferable state of affairs regarding Gödel, anonymity or misinterpretation. Which would Gödel have preferred? I'm going to indulge in 'the privileged position of the biographer' to presume I know the answer to the latter question, at least: Gödel, who was so passionately committed to the truth, would have far preferred utter oblivion to the falsifications of his theorems that have given him whatever fame he has in the non-mathematical world.

And what falsifications! He had meant his incompleteness theorems to prove the philosophical position to which he was, heart and soul, committed: mathematical Platonism, which is, in short, the belief that there is a human-independent mathematical reality that grounds our mathematical truths; mathematicians are in the business of discovering, rather than inventing, mathematics. His incompleteness theorems concerned the incompleteness of our man-made formal systems, not of mathematical truth, or our knowledge of it. He believed that mathematical reality and our knowledge of mathematical reality exceed the formal rules of formal systems. So unlike the view that says there is no truth apart from the truths we create for ourselves, so that the entire concept of truth disintegrates into a plurality of points of view, Gödel believed that truth – most paradigmatically, mathematical truth – subsists independently of any human point of view. If ever there was a man committed to the objectivity of truth, and to objective standards of rationality, it was Gödel. And so the usurpation of his theorems by postmodernists is ironic. Jean Cocteau wrote in 1926 that 'The worst tragedy for a poet is to be admired through being misunderstood.' For a logician, especially one with Gödel's delicate psychology, the tragedy is perhaps even greater.[7]

This tactic doesn't work with people who actually know something of Einstein, Heisenberg and Gödel – but what of it? How many people is that? And it does work with many who don't.

Asking unanswerable questions is an inconclusive but useful tactic. It doesn't permanently or physically silence the messenger in the way that execution, banishment and censorship do, but it may temporarily silence and divert. 'But *why* did all this happen? Why is there something rather than nothing? Why is there Mind? Why is there order? Why is there what looks like design even if you refuse to agree that it is design? Why are we here? What is our purpose? What does it all mean?' The fact that no one can answer such questions is taken by the pure of heart and limpid of mind to entail divine explanation. The fact that such explanation simply permits exactly the same questions to be asked all over again seems not to trouble the divinely inclined.

Looking for rival evidence, evidence that will support the opposite conclusions from the ones the searcher dislikes, looks at first blush like a perfectly legitimate move – like not even a move at all, but simply what enquirers and researchers and truth-seekers do: look for evidence. It looks as if we've left the territory of truth-denial and are back in the well-lit world of properly conducted research. But no. The trouble is that an enquirer who starts with a claim she wants to find evidence for is extremely likely to overlook disconfirming evidence.

This seems to be just what happened with Margaret Mead, for instance.

Mead went to graduate school in anthropology at a time when racist, eugenic and anti-immigrant ideas were at the height of their popularity in the USA, as we will see in more detail in Chapter 5. She was a student of Franz Boas, a pioneer of anthropology who spent much of his career struggling to counter such ideas. To cite just one example, his tenure as curator of anthropology at the American Museum of Natural History was roiled by disputes over the best way to display artefacts in the museum's Hall of Northwest Coast Indians, which opened in 1899. The traditional method was in a hierarchy of development, from simple to complex. Boas was strongly opposed to that method: he argued that to understand the meaning of objects, viewers needed to see them as their makers saw them, rather than in a scheme superimposed by outsiders. 'As always with Boas, details concealed a broader argument: in this case, against seeing human culture in evolutionary terms, rising from the "primitive" to a summit on which the inventors of the evolutionary scheme inevitably perched.'[8] The Northwest Coast Hall was arranged according to Boas's ideas – but Morris Jessup, the president of the museum, grumbled that he couldn't make head or tail of the exhibits, and in 1905 a collection of Peruvian artefacts was arranged in the old hierarchical pattern. Boas resigned, citing 'fundamental differences of opinion'.[9]

Mead was committed to the Boasian approach, and this fact shaped her early career, including her choice of dissertation subject and her approach to the fieldwork involved. Boas was a cultural determinist; his brand of anthropology was dominated by the idea that social conditioning shaped all human thought and behaviour. By the time Mead went to Samoa in 1925, Derek Freeman says in his *Margaret Mead and the Heretic*, she was a firm believer 'that human behaviour could be explained in purely cultural terms'. Cultural anthropology was becoming a thriving discipline but 'at the cost of becoming an ideology that, in an actively unscientific way, sought totally to exclude biology from the explanation of human behaviour'. Mead described this mission 'as a battle which she and other Boasians had had to fight'. Thus her writings about Samoa and other South Seas cultures 'had the explicit aim of confuting biological explanations of human behaviour and vindicating the doctrines of the Boasian school'.

In retrospect, Freeman points out, it is apparent that this approach – what we called looking for alternative evidence, that is, knowing in advance what one wants to find and then searching it out – 'is fundamentally at variance with the methods and values of science' and that Mead's commitment to supporting Boas's views 'led her to overlook evidence running counter to her beliefs'.[10]

A similar approach – similar in that it starts from a desired conclusion, then devises a way to get there, and then proceeds to carry out the plan – is that of seeking a rival explanation. If you don't like the theory that (as far as present knowledge can tell) best fits and explains the evidence, then you set to work and think up another. The names Duhem and Quine are useful to conjure with for this exercise, as is the phrase 'the underdetermination of theory by data'. It is always *possible* to think of alternative explanations for any set of data. The alternative explanations may be awkward, contorted, uneconomical and generally far-fetched; they may flout Ockham's razor and ignore norms of elegance, beauty, plausibility, avoidance of supernatural explanations and gods of the gaps; but if one is not deterred by such considerations, alternative explanations can be generated and made to 'fit'.

And of course many people are not deterred by such consider-ations: some because they're simply not aware of them, and would be indifferent if they were made aware; others because they are programmatically sceptical about them. Such norms are seen as themselves part of what is in dispute, so that they cannot be used to rule out alternative explanations without question-begging. If the norms of science as well as the explanations, and the kinds of explanation science generates, are precisely what is being 'problematized' and questioned then, the argument goes, they cannot be invoked to rebut such questioning and problematization. Sceptics about science and truth, anti-realists, postmodernists, gender and identity epistemologists and enemies of the Enlightenment project are indeed probing, questioning, criticizing these norms. (And, ironically, as everyone notices, they are doing it by means of rational argument, and they want and expect their arguments to be accepted and taken as true, so the despised problematized norms immediately slide back in by the rear door.)

So, at the price of offering contorted implausible accounts, alternative explanations can be made to fit – sort of – in a Procrustean, glass slipper sense of 'fit'. Clearly to many people the desire and need to come up with a more pleasing, less disconcerting explanation is vastly more important than any lumpishness and roughness in the explanation itself. But to those for whom the truth matters more than a pleasing account, the contortions involved in the fit are almost always a dead giveaway that the explanation in question is not the right one, and it is not merely imperfect or unattractive but rather entirely worthless.

In fact, the contortions are a giveaway not only that the explanation is not the right one but that something is badly wrong with the method of generating the explanation, that things are back to front, that the enquirer has started, not with a desire to produce an explanation, but with a desire to produce a particular explanation, or a particular kind of explanation. The enquirer has started with stipulations. The stipulations may have been so deeply implicit as to be below the level of awareness, but they were nonetheless binding for that. And they were the wrong kinds of stipulations. Not those that dictate, for instance, that the explanation must fit the evidence, must not conceal evidence that does not fit, must not alter the evidence to fit the explanation, and the like, but rather that the explanation must be in harmony with some cherished belief or goal or commitment of the enquirer. The explanation must not entail or imply that there is no God, or that God is superfluous, or that humans share a common descent with other animals, or that the Bible is not an accurate account of geology or the origin of species or history, or that acquired characteristics cannot be inherited, or that free will is an illusion, or that the mind is what the brain does, or that human nature is strongly shaped by its genetic makeup.

The naturalist Philip Gosse, who was also a member of the Plymouth Brethren (a Christian sect fundamentalist even by nineteenth-century standards) is a fascinating example of this sort of prior-stipulation-generated explanation. His son Edmund's memoir *Father and Son* gives a poignant and shrewd account, which it is worth quoting at length:

> So, through my Father's brain, in that year of scientific crisis, 1857, there rushed two kinds of thought, each absorbing, each convincing, yet totally irreconcilable. There is a peculiar agony in the paradox that truth has two forms, each of them indisputable, yet each antagonistic to the other. It was this discovery, that there were two theories of physical life, each of which was true, but the truth of each incompatible with the truth of the other, which shook the spirit of my Father with perturbation. It was not, really, a paradox, it was a fallacy, if he could only have known it, but he allowed the turbid volume of superstition to drown the delicate stream of reason. He took one step in the service of truth, and then he drew back in an agony, and accepted the servitude of error ...
>
> My Father's attitude towards the theory of natural selection was critical in his career, and oddly enough, it exercised an immense influence on my own experience as a child. Let it be admitted at once, mournful as the admission is, that every instinct in his intelligence went out at first to greet the new light. It had hardly done so, when a recollection of the opening chapter of 'Genesis' checked it at the outset. He consulted with Carpenter, a great investigator, but one who was fully as incapable as himself of remodelling his ideas with regard to the old, accepted hypotheses. They both determined, on various grounds, to have nothing to do with the terrible theory, but to hold steadily to the law of the fixity of species. It was exactly at this juncture that we left London, and the slight and occasional but always extremely salutary personal intercourse with men of scientific leaning which my Father had enjoyed at the British Museum and at the

Royal Society came to an end ... My Father, after long reflection, prepared a theory of his own, which, as he fondly hoped, would take the wind out of Lyell's sails, and justify geology to godly readers of 'Genesis'. It was, very briefly, that there had been no gradual modification of the surface of the earth, or slow development of organic forms, but that when the catastrophic act of creation took place, the world presented, instantly, the structural appearance of a planet on which life had long existed.

The theory, coarsely enough, and to my Father's great indignation, was defined by a hasty press as being this – that God hid the fossils in the rocks in order to tempt geologists into infidelity. In truth, it was the logical and inevitable conclusion of accepting, literally, the doctrine of a sudden act of creation; it emphasised the fact that any breach in the circular course of nature could be conceived only on the supposition that the object created bore false witness to past processes, which had never taken place. For instance, Adam would certainly possess hair and teeth and bones in a condition which it must have taken many years to accomplish, yet he was created full-grown yesterday. He would certainly – though Sir Thomas Browne denied it – display an 'omphalos', yet no umbilical cord had ever attached him to a mother.

Never was a book cast upon the waters with greater anticipations of success than was this curious, this obstinate, this fanatical volume. My Father lived in a fever of suspense, waiting for the tremendous issue. This 'Omphalos' of his, he thought, was to bring all the turmoil of scientific speculation to a close, fling geology into the arms of Scripture, and make the lion eat grass with the lamb ... In the course of that dismal winter, as the post began to bring in private letters, few and chilly, and public reviews, many and scornful, my Father looked in vain for the approval of the churches, and in vain for the acquiescence of the scientific societies, and in vain for the gratitude of those 'thousands of thinking persons', which he had rashly assured himself of receiving. As his reconciliation of Scripture statements and geological deductions was welcomed nowhere, as Darwin continued silent, and the youthful Huxley was scornful, and even Charles Kingsley, from whom my Father had expected the most instant appreciation, wrote that he could not 'give up the painful and slow conclusion of five and twenty years' study of geology, and believe that God has written on the rocks one enormous and superfluous lie', – as all this happened or failed to happen, a gloom, cold and dismal, descended upon our morning teacups.[11]

This is the crux of the dispute. This is where the two sides always peel apart. What should trump what. Should rational enquiry, sound evidence, norms of accuracy, logical inference trump human needs, desires, fears, hopes? Or should our wishes and beliefs, politics and morality, dreams and visions be allowed to shape our decisions about what constitutes good evidence, what criteria determine whether an explanation is supported by evidence or not, what is admissable and what isn't?

This crux is never finally settled; it's always with us. It's a fork in the path we find ourselves at many times a day, like a recurring landscape in a dream. That's inevitable, because what is important to us is important to us. The truth is important to us, but so are our needs and desires and hopes and fears. Without them we wouldn't even recognize ourselves. Without them, we think, we would merely be something like an adding machine. An adding machine can get at the truth, given the right input, but it doesn't care. We want the truth but we also want to care – wanting the truth is indeed inseparable from caring. We want it, we care about it, it matters, and so do various other things we want and care about, some of which are threatened by the truth. So we're stuck, and keep arriving back at the fork in the path again.

But we have to choose. Even though our choosing doesn't make the crux go away, even though we still have to go on making micro-choices over and over again, still, we have to choose which fork in the path we are going to take. If we don't, we have a tendency not to notice the crux when it does appear. If we've never bothered to decide that truth matters and that it shouldn't be subject to our wishes – that, in short, wishful thinking is bad thinking – then we are likely to be far less aware of the tension. We simply allow ourselves, without much worry or reflection, to assume that the way humans want the world to be is the way the world is, more or less by definition – and endemic confusion and muddle is the result.

Religion and related modes of thinking such as New Age, Wicca, paganism, the vaguely named 'spirituality', are where this outcome is most obvious. Public discourse features talk of God-shaped holes, of a deep human need for 'faith', of the longing for transcendence, of the despair and cosmic loneliness that results when God is doubted, and the like; and such talk has a tendency to be prescriptive rather than descriptive: to say, or imply, not 'people are happier when they believe in a deity, how sad there seems to be so little reason to think such a belief is true', but rather, 'people are happier when they believe in a deity, therefore it's wicked to say the deity isn't there', without apparently stopping to notice that there may be reasons to prefer true beliefs to false ones.

What reasons? There are many. One is that truth is something of an all-or-nothing proposition. It is intimately related to concepts such as consistency, thoroughness, universal applicability, and the like. If one decides that truth doesn't matter in one area, what is to prevent one from deciding it doesn't matter in any, in all?

It is surely of the nature of truth that it has to be all of a piece. Its norms have to apply here as well as there, if they are to apply at all. That's why relativism about truth is always self-undermining. If we say 'there is no truth, truth is an illusion, a myth, a construct, a mystification', then that statement is not true – so there is truth then. If we say 'your truth is as true as mine' then you can say 'my truth is that your truth is not true', and round we go.

Such reasons are especially cogent as soon as we leave the comfort of our own minds and enter the public realm; as soon as we start influencing each other, by talking, arguing, persuading, communicating – and above all, by teaching. Our secret, private, internal thoughts may not matter all that much. Elizabeth I herself – she who cut off the hand of John Stubbs for writing a tract – disavowed any intention of peering into people's minds. But how we influence each other, what we teach – by writing, by journalism, by talking on the radio, on platforms, in churches and mosques, in classrooms – that does matter. If we are going to influence people, it's important that we get it right.

Which brings us to the subject of this book, which is various (but related) forms of scepticism and relativism about truth and the possibility of knowledge. There are different branches of this phenomenon, and different labels. Postmodernism, epistemic relativism, anti-realism, anti-foundationalism, neopragmatism, feminist epistemology, the strong programme in the sociology of science and knowledge, postcolonialism, and so on. The central idea is the one we've been stalking and creeping up on all this time: scepticism and doubt about the reality, meaning, possibility, importance of truth, and the tendency, which truth-scepticism makes so much easier, to distort and shape truth to favour particular viewpoints

It's an old idea, this central one, as we will see in Chapter 2, but it has had a renewal of popularity and influence in some branches of the humanities and social sciences in the last three or four decades. Many books and articles have appeared, raising an eyebrow and smiling an incredulous smile at concepts such as rationality, well-conducted enquiry, evidence, inference, warrant, justification, the Enlightenment project, universalism, science and truth. Suspicion of metanarratives, hostility to totalizing projects, condemnation of universalism as a tool of colonialism, identification of knowledge with power, distrust of binary oppositions, resistance to hegemonic discourses, decentring, problematization, interrogation of authority, hierarchies, logocentrism, phallogocentrism – are all part of the arsenal. Some interesting, fruitful and possibly even true ideas have emerged from all this, but there have also been many extremely bad, silly, ill-founded and harmful ones. Those are the ones we want to have a look at.

But does it really matter? Is it worth bothering about? Academic fashions come and go. Dons and professors are always coming up with some New Big Thing, and then getting old and doddering off to the great library in the sky, while new dons and professors hatch new big things, some more and some less silly than others. Casaubon had his key to all mythologies, Derrida had his, someone will have a new one tomorrow; what of it?

Yes, is our answer; it does matter. It matters for various pragmatic, instrumental reasons. Meera Nanda discusses in *Prophets Facing Backward* the way Hindu fundamentalists in India have drawn on postmodernist scepticism and hostility to science in 'Hinduizing' Indian science, education, textbooks and the like. Richard Evans argues in his book *In Defense of History* that postmodernist scepticism about historical evidence and truth, along with valuable insights, also has dangerous implications.

> Nazi Germany seemed to postmodernism's critics to be the point at which an end to hyperrelativism was called for … There is in fact a massive, carefully empirical literature on the Nazi extermination of the Jews. Clearly, to regard it as fictional, or unreal, or no nearer to historical reality than, say, the work of the 'revisionists' who deny that Auschwitz ever happened at all is simply wrong. Here is an issue where evidence really counts, and can be used to establish the essential facts. Auschwitz was not a discourse. It trivializes mass murder to see it as a text. The gas chambers were not a piece of rhetoric. Auschwitz was indeed inherently a tragedy and cannot be seen as either a comedy or a farce. And if this is true of Auschwitz, then it must be true at least to some degree of other past happenings, events, institutions as well.[12]

That passage is in a book published in 1997. Three years later Evans saw his point enacted in a court of law.

> In the David Irving libel trial held two years ago, in which I served as an expert witness for the High Court in London, Irving was suing Penguin Books and their author Deborah Lipstadt for calling him a Holocaust denier and a falsifier of history. It was not difficult to show that Irving had claimed on many occasions that no Jews were killed in gas chambers at the Auschwitz concentration camp. He argued in the courtroom, however, that his claim was supported by the historical evidence. The defence therefore brought forward the world's leading expert on Auschwitz, Robert Jan Van Pelt, to present the evidence that showed that hundreds of thousands of Jews were in fact killed in this way. Van Pelt

examined eyewitness testimony from camp officials and inmates, he looked at photographic evidence of the physical remains of the camp, and he studied contemporary documents such as plans, blueprints, letters, equipment orders, architectural designs, reports and so on. Each of these three kinds of evidence, as the judge concluded, had its flaws and its problems. But all three converged along the same lines, creating an overwhelming probability that Irving was wrong.

Just as important as this was the fact that it was possible to demonstrate that Irving's historical works deliberately falsified the documentary evidence in order to lend plausibility to his preconceived arguments, principally his belief that Hitler was, as he said on one occasion, 'probably the best friend the Jews ever had in the Third Reich'. Falsifying documents involved not just leaving words out from quotes but even putting extra words in to change the meaning. For example, quoting an order from Himmler that a 'Jew-transport from Berlin' to the East should not be annihilated as if it were a general order that no Jews at all, anywhere, were to be killed, by the simple expedients of adding an 'e' to the German word *Transport*, making it plural, and omitting the words 'from Berlin', and hoping that other researchers wouldn't trouble to check the source, or if they did, wouldn't be able to read the handwriting (which is actually very clear and unambiguous). Or by adding the word 'All' to the note of a judge at the Nuremberg Trial in 1946 on the testimony of an Auschwitz survivor which actually said 'this I do not believe', after a small part of her testimony, to make it look as if he did not believe any of it. If we actually believed that documents could say anything we wanted them to, then none of this would actually matter, and it would not be possible to expose historical fraud for what it really is.[13]

There are also reasons beyond the pragmatic and instrumental why truth matters, why it can be seen as an inherent good. They are not conclusive, knock-down, irrefutable reasons, they are not mathematical proofs, but they are reasons. We will discuss some in the final chapter. But for now we will content ourselves with some thoughts about what human beings are, and why, being what they are, they should consider truth a very important value, and considering it such, treat it accordingly.

Looked at in that light, the thought that leaps out at us is this: that humans are the only entities in the entire universe, for all we know, who have the capacity to make truth their object. The other needs and wishes, the ones that can conflict with truth, the needs and wishes for contentment, happiness, comfort, feelings of security and safety and being protected, are ones that other beings can want and strive for after a fashion. But truth? No. We, by this strange provocative contingent accident of natural selection, have the kind of brain that can conceptualize reality as existing independent of us, and the possibility that we can discover what it is, along with the possibility that we can try to do that and fail, that we can think we've discovered it and be wrong, that we can discover part of it and be at a loss about the rest, and so on.

So one intrinsic reason for thinking we ought to respect the truth, and try to find out what it is, which entails not fudging it whenever we don't like what we find, which entails deciding firmly *in advance* that we will put it first and all other considerations second – one reason for all this is simply that we can, and that as far as we know we are the only ones who can. We can, so we ought to. It would be such a waste not to. If only as a sort of tribute to the remarkable accident of natural selection; to the staggering amazing chain of being: from nothing to something, to life, to intelligence, to truth-seeking.

And then, truth can be seen as a major part of the human heritage. Along with the pyramids and the Great Wall and King's College Chapel, the cumulative gathering up of true knowledge about the world is something that belongs to all human beings across time – particularly of course into the future. It doesn't belong to any of us in particular, to any one generation, to any mere short-lived *set* of humans, but to all of us. No one brief generation has the right to tamper with it for the sake of its own ephemeral satisfactions. Think of the Bamiyan Buddhas. How disgusting it was, and is, that a band of fundamentalist thugs should dare to destroy something that ought to have belonged to all humans across time as well as across space. The truth is a Bamiyan Buddha. It belongs to everyone, not anyone. No one has a right to destroy or distort or damage it for petty temporary political reasons.

2 Truth, Doubt and the Philosophers

By convention hot, by convention cold; in reality atoms and void.

(Democritus)

Dareios in the course of his reign summoned those of the Hellenes who were present in his land, and asked them for what price they would consent to eat up their fathers when they died; and they answered that for no price would they do so. After this Dareios summoned those Indians who are called Callatians, who eat their parents, and asked them in presence of the Hellenes ... for what payment they would consent to consume with fire the bodies of their fathers when they died; and they cried out aloud and bade him keep silence from such words. Thus then these things are established by usage, and I think that Pindar spoke rightly in his verse, when he said that 'of all things custom is king'.[1]

(Herodotus, *The History*, 3.38)

Herodotus is making an observation here about the relativity of cultural norms which had caught the attention of many Greeks, especially Athenians, in the fifth century BCE. Increasing contact with other civilizations through war, immigration and trade had brought with it an awareness that behaviour is rooted in custom (*nomos*), and is not straightforwardly a function of human nature (*physis*). This seems to have been a new idea; at any rate, it was much discussed by philosophers and playwrights as well as newfangled writers such as Herodotus.

Herodotus was fascinated by this discovery of the variability of custom; it is the subject of much of his vast, gossipy, garrulous book. He was enthralled by the foreign customs of the Persians, and by the Persians' own openness to foreign customs:

> The Persians welcome foreign customs more than any other people. For instance, they decided that Median dress was more beautiful than their own, and so they wear it. They wear Egyptian breastplates for their wars. Wherever they learn of enjoyments of all sorts, they adopt them for their own practice.[2]

Contrast this with the Scythians (a people who lived in what is now southern Russia): 'These people dreadfully avoid the use of foreign customs, and especially those of the Greeks ...'[3] The fact that people have different customs seems to indicate that they can vary their customs, which can come as a surprise to people who are used to thinking of their own customs as permanent and unquestionable, like 'rocks, and stones, and trees'. The fact that customs can be changed *can* (though it doesn't have to) lead to the thought that perhaps they ought to be, that – as the Persians must have thought when they adopted the Medians' pretty clothes – different ways might be better ways, and therefore might be worth adopting. It can also lead to the thought that even if our customs are better for us, still their customs may be better for them; in other words, cultural relativism.

Certainly a similar thought struck Montaigne 20 centuries later. He was as enthralled and mentally stimulated by the unfamiliar customs of the peoples of the New World as Herodotus was by those of the Scythians and Egyptians. His essay 'On the Cannibals' is based on his reading of travellers' reports and also the conversation of an acquaintance who had spent ten or twelve years in America.

> I find ... that there is nothing savage or barbarous about those peoples, but that every man calls barbarous anything he is not accustomed to; it is indeed the case that we have no other criterion of truth or right-reason than the example and form of the opinions and customs of our own

country. There we always find the perfect religion, the perfect polity, the most developed and perfect way of doing anything![4]

Such ideas can also open the door to further thoughts that some – Plato for one – find alarming and threatening. If customs are local, and therefore malleable, maybe so are other things. Religion. Morality. Knowledge. Maybe nothing is actually better or worse than anything else, but merely different. Maybe we could do everything in exactly the opposite way to the way we do it now, and it would make no difference to anything.

What do I know?

The early Greek philosophers were certainly concerned with the problem of knowledge, with how and if we know what we know, with the obscurity of truth and the consequent difficulty of knowing when we have or have not found it, with whether we can ever be absolutely certain of anything. Socrates described, whether ironically or double-ironically, his surprise when the Delphic oracle declared him the wisest man in Athens. (It must have been like an unexpected phone call from Stockholm.) But then he figured out (he claimed, with or without tongue in cheek) that it was because he was the only one who knew he didn't know anything.

Hellenistic philosophers developed this dictum of Socrates' into two kinds of scepticism. The first, Academic scepticism, argues that no knowledge is possible; the second, Pyrrhonian, argues that there is not enough evidence to decide if knowledge is possible and therefore one ought to suspend judgement.[5] Richard Popkin, in his influential *History of Scepticism*, describes the Renaissance revival of interest in Pyrrhonian scepticism via the writing of Sextus Empiricus (c. 200 CE), and the coincidence of that revival with the crisis of knowledge brought about by Luther's escalating challenges to the authority of the Church. One of the central disagreements of the

Reformation, Popkin points out, was that over 'the proper standard of religious knowledge'. This argument, he continues, 'raised one of the classical problems of the Greek Pyrrhonists, the problem of the criterion of truth'.[6] Popkin quotes Sextus Empiricus on this problem:

> ... in order to decide the dispute which has arisen about the criterion, we must possess an accepted criterion by which we shall be able to judge the dispute; and in order to possess an accepted criterion, the dispute about the criterion must first be decided. And when the argument thus resolves itself to a form of circular reasoning the discovery of the criterion becomes impracticable ...[7]

The problem is obvious enough in the endless arguments between Luther and the Church. Luther said, essentially, 'Why should we believe the Church, the popes, the clergy? We should believe Scripture with the guidance of our conscience and inner knowledge instead.' And the Church replied 'Why should anyone else believe Luther's conscience and inner knowledge? That way anarchy lies.' And so they wrangled on, for decades and centuries, with burnings, massacres and wars.

Scepticism was a useful refuge or escape-route from this futile dead-end wrangle. As Popkin and Avrum Stoll put it in *Skeptical Philosophy for Everyone*, the Pyrrhonist suspension of belief or *epochē* 'is consistent with a kind of passive acceptance of the world; one lives in the world, acts in it, takes it as it is without reflection. *Epochē* is important because it is the first step toward *ataraxia* – a special kind of mental tranquillity.'[8] Montaigne knew how to value *ataraxia*, though he never actually gave up on reflection. He saw much violence and cruelty in the French wars of religion, and he was both irritated and amused by human certainties, which he mocked throughout the essays and systematically undermined in 'The Apology for Raymond Sebond'. The conclusion he drew from thoroughgoing scepticism was a fideist one of a sort: nobody can know anything for certain, therefore one might as well conform to the local custom and religion. His stance is so teasingly paradoxical and shifting that readers and scholars still disagree on whether he was a genuine believer or a politely conforming non-believer. Either way, his influence worked in both directions, as Popkin describes:

> Whether Montaigne was trying to undermine Christianity or defend it, he could have made the same *non sequitur* that he did, namely, because all is doubt, therefore one ought to accept Christianity on faith alone. Such a claim was made by Hume and Voltaire, apparently in bad faith, and by Pascal and Kierkegaard, apparently in good faith. The type of Christian Pyrrhonism stated by Montaigne and his disciples was taken by some Church leaders as the best of theology, and by others as rank atheism.[9]

The Cartesian turn

Although Montaigne might have found the Pyrrhonist *epochē* a satisfactory response to the problem of the missing criterion of truth, René Descartes did not. In *Discourse on Method*, he tells how in his youth he had been haunted by the spectre of uncertainty:

> I found myself hampered by so many doubts and errors that the only benefit of my efforts to become an educated person seemed to be the increasing discovery of my own ignorance. And yet I had been in one of the most famous schools in all Europe ... The age in which we live seemed to me to be no less flourishing, no less fertile in good minds, than any of its predecessors. And so, in the end, I allowed myself the liberty of taking my own predicament as universal, and of concluding that nowhere in the world was there any knowledge professed of the kind I had been encouraged to expect.[10]

Descartes' response to this situation was to seek out the grounds upon which truth might be secured. Thus, in his *Meditations on First Philosophy*, he makes use of a method of radical doubt with the aim of establishing at least one certain belief which could then form the foundations of knowledge. Radical doubt meant just that; as

Descartes put it, 'the slightest suspicion of a doubt will be enough to make me reject any one of my beliefs'.[11]

Descartes' argument here is one of the most famous in the history of philosophy. He succeeds in showing that we might be mistaken about particular sense data; that it is possible to throw the whole of our sense experience into doubt – we could, for example, be dreaming, yet not realize it; and, more radically, that it is possible that there is nothing at all behind our sense experiences – we might simply have been deceived about it all by an evil demon.

However, this process also shows that there is one resilient belief. No matter how rigorously we apply the method of doubt, it is not possible to doubt that we exist; the very act of doubting means that there must be an 'I' which is doing the doubting. This is Descartes' famous *cogito*:

> In persuading myself that there was nothing at all in the world, neither heaven nor earth, no minds and no bodies, did I not also persuade myself that I did not exist? Certainly not, for there can be no doubt that I exist in the very act of persuading myself, or indeed of thinking anything at all ... after due thought and scrupulous reflection, I must conclude that the proposition, *I am, I exist*, is true of necessity every time I state it or conceive it in my mind.[12]

However, Descartes now has a problem. Having established the existence of a thinking entity (if it has been established), how does he get the rest of the world back? The short answer is that he can't; at least, not to the satisfaction of a modern philosopher. His attempt involves employing a version of the ontological argument in order to demonstrate the existence of God, and then to argue that since God is not a deceiver, we are not systematically misled about those things we perceive clearly. It is then fairly easy to get back certain of our beliefs about the external world.

The interesting thing from our point of view is the legacy which Descartes bequeathed to philosophy with this argument. Clearly, in one way, the Cartesian search for certainty and inviolable truth is antithetical to both scepticism and relativism. It was Descartes' view that reason is universal, and therefore, in principle at least, the truths which it uncovers are available to all. However, by dividing reality into inner (i.e., the mind) and outer bits, where it is the job of the inner bit to 'represent' the outer bit, he created a crack through which both scepticism and relativism could and would come crashing through.

A brief diversion

This division of the world into inner and outer bits, where the former – the conscious, maybe rational, bit – somehow comes to knowledge of the latter, results in difficult, enduring and quite possibly insoluble philosophical problems.[13] It is possible to get a sense of these by stripping them of their complicated philosophical clothes, to consider them instead as the kinds of puzzles which might be the subject of a more sophisticated than usual Hollywood movie.

Consider, then, that human beings are limited, evolved organisms; their brains, made of physical stuff, process data which come in from the outside world via their sense organs. These data, having been turned into information, allow humans to move around and interact with their environment. Genes which construct brains that allow humans to do this successfully are passed on more often than their less successful alternatives. This whole process is, as far as we know, driven by determinate, physical laws.

The philosophical problem in all this is that it is not clear what grounds we have for thinking our brains are telling us stories which accurately represent the world, rather than stories which merely help us to survive in the world. To put this in simple Darwinian terms, we have evolved to survive, not to know the truth about the world. Added to this, there is a huge unsolved puzzle here about how it is that physical things can know anything at all; or, to put this more starkly, after Colin McGinn, how it is that 'meat' can know anything at all.[14]

A possible objection to this line of argument is to claim that while it is a logical *possibility* that our brains process data in such a way that we might be misled about the nature of the world, there is no good evidence to suggest that this is in fact the case. This is a strong argument, not least because it calls Descartes on his idea that knowledge requires the absence of all doubt. However, there are two responses to the argument, both of which are troubling.

The first is that there is plenty of evidence which suggests that the brain does structure our experience in ways that can be misleading. Here's psychiatrist Robin Murray on the auditory hallucinations which accompany schizophrenia:

> I can think of a chap who was in the middle of doing a BSc in psychology when he started hallucinating ... He heard voices speaking to him. He thought that other people were out to harm him. When he recovered, after getting treatment, he said that it was amazing that there he was, a psychologist, and he knew all about the symptoms of schizophrenia, and when it happened to him it never crossed his mind that he might be suffering from the illness. He knew they were out to get him. He knew that these voices were real. Presumably it is something about the nature and intensity of the experiences which makes them so hard to resist. But we also now know from brain imaging that when sufferers are hallucinating they are activating not only the area in the brain which produces inner speech, which is called Broca's area, but also the auditory cortex in the temporal lobe which is normally involved in processing external speech. The sufferer is tricked into believing that the words are coming from an external source because they are being processed by the same neural system that we use when listening to external speech.[15]

The obvious response here is to claim that while damaged brains might mislead us, normal functioning brains do not. Unfortunately, the evidence does not support this claim. The philosopher Edmund Husserl, who had a particular interest in the nature of conscious experience, was committed to the somewhat paradoxical view that consciousness constitutes the objects to which it is directed and yet the external world still has a reality of its own. Husserl's idea seems to be – though it is a matter of ongoing scholarly debate – that what comes in from the outside is not sufficient to determine our consciousness of it. This general idea is a bit mysterious until you've seen something like this:

A BIRD	ONCE
IN THE	UPON A
THE HAND	A TIME

At first sight, most people will read these statements as 'a bird in the hand' and 'once upon a time'. However, this is not what they actually say. Read them again if that isn't clear (and if it still isn't, point at each word!). Our perception is distorted here because our familiarity with these phrases – or, more accurately, with the phrases which these are designed to mimic – creates an expectation which our perceptual systems fulfil. According to Adelbert Ames's transactionalist account of perception, this kind of perceptual 'filling in' is not unusual; retinal images are ambiguous, so our perceptual systems necessarily infer from past experience, and sometimes they get things wrong.

While these demonstrations of the fallibility of perception are illuminating and fun, they will not convince anybody that our brains *systematically* mislead us about the nature of the world. It will be objected that we should expect occasional mistakes; that there are lots of mechanisms available to allow us to check the veracity of our perceptual experiences (not least, we can hold them up against the experiences of other people); and that the very fact that we can identify mistakes shows that our brains work just fine most of the time.

This counter-argument is both absolutely right, and yet inadequate to see off the sceptical challenge. It is inadequate because there is a second response one can make to the original argument (that there's no good evidence to show we are misled about the nature of the world). Put simply, one can object to this argument that it misses the force of the sceptical challenge. In order to talk about evidence, about the rational assessment of arguments, and so on, it is necessary to presuppose precisely what is being denied; namely, that we have grounds to think that the brain – just conscious meat, after all – is the kind of entity which is able to generate accurate knowledge about the world.

If people are genuinely committed to the view that an organic, mechanistic entity, which evolved under survival and reproductive imperatives, is an unlikely source of knowledge about the world; if they further think that what we take to be truths about the world are actually convenient stories designed to keep us alive, but stories which only function properly if they seem to be warranted; then they're not going to be convinced that they're wrong by an appeal to evidence which presupposes that the brain *is* a reliable source of knowledge.[16]

Since this is the Hollywood version of a certain kind of sceptical challenge, it would be wrong to think that it is a knock-down argument. It isn't. However, it does flag up some of the difficulties which emerge when one begins to examine how a sceptical argument might be constructed. It also serves to bring to the surface a paradox which is attached to certain versions of both scepticism and relativism.

This paradox emerges out of what philosopher David Stove has called the 'Ishmael effect', which refers to those occasions where philosophical arguments make exceptions of themselves.[17] The point here is that it seems that the sceptical challenge outlined above only works if it makes an exception of itself. Consider, for example, that in this version of it we have made certain empirical claims – about the nature of brains, evolution, perception, and so on – which we only have warrant to assert if we think that there *is* a way to distinguish between true statements and false statements. It would have been possible, of course, to have put together a sceptical argument which didn't rely so heavily on empirical evidence; but, even so, as Simon Blackburn points out, 'the idea that there is something self-undermining about the relativist or sceptical tradition dies hard'.[18]

A universal reason?

Johann Georg Hamann, though hardly a household name now, was perhaps the leading counter-Enlightenment thinker of his day. Isaiah Berlin described him thus:

> … the most passionate, consistent, extreme and implacable enemy of the Enlightenment and, in particular, of all forms of rationalism of his time … His influence, direct and indirect, upon the romantic revolt against universalism and scientific method in any guise was considerable and perhaps crucial.[19]

The Enlightenment, which, according to Kant, marked the 'emergence of man from his self-imposed infancy', emphasized the universality of reason, and the multiple contexts of reason's applicability. Thus, a thinker such as Voltaire, for example, thought that human beings could employ reason in order to act, to solve problems, to find out about the world, to examine their religious beliefs, and to progress morally. The Enlightenment project was universalizing in its intent; reason was thought to be everywhere sovereign over the claims of custom, locality and community.

It is to this extension of reason that Hamann objected in *Socratic Memorabilia*, his first work directed against the Enlightenment. His concern here was to demonstrate that religious faith is impervious to the criticisms levelled at it by reason. To do this, he turned David Hume's 'mitigated scepticism' against itself, arguing that if our beliefs cannot be grounded in reason, as he took Hume to have claimed, then equally they cannot be threatened by reason.[20] Moreover, if our everyday beliefs are ultimately based on a quasi-religious leap of faith, then surely such a leap is justified in the religious sphere.

Hamann's attack on reason and the Enlightenment became more pronounced in his later works. Specifically, he insisted that reason was embedded in particular linguistic, historical and social contexts. In Frederick Beiser's words, reason 'proves to be not a special kind of faculty existing in some Platonic or noumenal realm but only a specific manner of speaking, writing and acting in concrete cultural circumstances'.[21]

In her book *Relativism*, Maria Baghramian argues that Hamann's work can be seen as a precursor of modern relativism in two ways. First, his denial that there was an objective order from which it is possible to derive universal truths and values drove the 'romantic revolt', which was a stimulus for much of the antipathy which philosophers such as Nietzsche felt towards the universalizing tendencies of 'Western metaphysics'. Second, his ideas about language, his view that reason and rationality are themselves embedded in language, are similar to modern epistemic and linguistic relativism. Thus, Baghramian concludes that

> Hamann's analysis of language and meaning foreshadows the argument of contemporary relativists who deny the possibility of access to an external point of view from which to compare and criticise different worldviews and value-systems and who emphasise the need for criteria internal to a language or way of life for understanding and evaluating various belief-systems.[22]

Although people talk too easily of work 'foreshadowing' or 'anticipating' other work,[23] in this case there is indeed a striking similarity – though almost certainly it isn't a matter of direct influence – between the ideas of Hamann and those of somebody like Ludwig Wittgenstein.[24]

Ludwig Wittgenstein and the 'linguistic turn'

It is well known that Wittgenstein's ideas about language changed radically between his early and later work. There is, nevertheless, one thought common to both periods: that philosophy 'is a battle against the bewitchment of our intelligence by means of language'.[25]

For the later Wittgenstein, part of this battle involved ensuring that we didn't take language to function as he argued it did in the

Tractatus, the great work of his early period. Particularly, he had come to think that the idea that language is a determinate system, within which simple propositions stand for states of affairs of the world (the so-called pictorial theory of meaning), was fundamentally misconceived. His new ideas about language and meaning were mainly developed in the posthumously published *Philosophical Investigations*. In this work, Wittgenstein set out to show that language gains its meaning from the way that it is used: 'For a *large* class of cases – though not for all – in which we employ the word "meaning" it can be defined thus: the meaning of a word is its use in the language.'[26] Thus, for example, the phrase 'I love you, too' means something entirely different when said in response to an insult from what it means if it is said to a lover in a tender moment. Its meaning is inextricably tied to the context in which it is used, and to the goals and intentions of the people involved in the communicative exchange.

Linked to this idea is the notion of a 'language-game'; how words function, and therefore their meaning, is dependent upon the 'game' being played. Wittgenstein mentioned, as examples of language-games: giving orders and obeying them, reporting an event, speculating about an event, putting together a hypothesis, joke-telling, cursing, and story-telling. The idea of the language-game brings into focus the fact that language is always linked to a particular 'form of life'.

This notion of a form of life is central to Wittgenstein's account of meaning; broadly speaking, it refers to the background context, with its biological, social and cultural aspects, which is presupposed in particular uses of language.[27] A. C. Grayling has explained this as well as anybody:

> ... it is the underlying consensus of linguistic and nonlinguistic behaviour, assumptions, practices, traditions, and natural propensities which humans, as social beings, share with one another, and which is therefore presupposed in the language they use; language is woven into that pattern of human activity and character, and meaning is conferred on its expressions by the shared outlook and nature of its users.[28]

Perhaps the key point for our purposes is that there is nothing beyond a form of life to explain or justify our use of particular concepts; there is no Platonic realm to fix the meaning – or indeed, the truth – of our utterances.

> The form of life is the frame of reference we learn to work within when trained in the language of our community; learning that language is thus learning the outlook, assumptions, and practices with which that language is inseparably bound and from which its expressions get their meaning.[29]

Wittgenstein puts it thus: 'What has to be accepted, the given, is – so one could say – *forms of life*.'[30]

For thinkers inclined towards relativism, this kind of stuff is a gift. Wittgenstein seems to be suggesting that it is only possible to determine the truth or otherwise of propositions from within particular language-games or forms of life. Even more than this, the notion of truth itself only makes sense in the same restricted sense; there is no view from nowhere which will give us access to an objective reality that in some way exists outside our attempts to grasp it in language.

However, this is philosophy, so no doubt Wittgenstein scholars all around the world flinch whenever they hear this kind of thing. But, in quite a strong sense, their flinching is beside the point. It is their job to worry about the nuances of Wittgenstein's account. But other people have other agendas, and it just is the case, rightly or wrongly, that Wittgenstein has been taken to be a relativist; that he has inspired other self-consciously relativistic accounts; and that he provides aid and comfort to those people who employ relativistic arguments, even if these arguments are not explicitly Wittgensteinian in form.

Consider, for example, that Wittgenstein stresses the lived, communal and shared nature of a form of life. It is no wonder that anthropologists who wish to challenge the political and cultural hegemony of the West will find this an attractive idea (especially if it is stripped of its philosophical complexity). It is just very easy to employ this kind of argument in order to demonstrate that the 'knowledges' produced by indigenous people are every bit as valid, 'in their own way', as the knowledge produced by Western science. And even if Wittgenstein's ideas are being misapplied, it is not clear that he would have good grounds for complaint, because, after all, it is only a small step from arguing that words gain their meaning through their use to the claim that so do philosophical theories.

Science under threat?

Peter Winch, a philosopher in the mould of the later Wittgenstein, argued in his article 'Understanding a primitive society' that rationality itself (i.e., the rules of logic, the standards of justified belief, modes of inferences, and the like) is a culturally embedded phenomenon. He went on to claim that there is therefore little point in trying to understand the beliefs of a culture which is radically alien to the Western scientific tradition in terms of the standards and conventions of that tradition: one would just run slap bang into a fundamental incommensurability. If Winch is right, then clearly there are implications for the way that anthropology goes about its business. But, perhaps more significantly, this incommensurability also says something important about the nature of science.

To put it simply, it is possible to see science as a form of life, with its own set of rules, practices and linguistic conventions. At first thought, it might seem that there is nothing particularly worrying about this idea. After all, one can imagine even the hardest-nosed scientist agreeing that science has its own particular way of doing things. But, on second thought, it becomes clear that this idea has implications for the status of scientific truths, and that these implications run contrary to the self-image of science. The threat is not scepticism; the criteria which allow it to be determined whether a proposition is true or false are well established within the scientific form of life. The threat is, rather, relativism. Put simply, if the scientific form of life runs up against an alternative, incommensurate form of life, perhaps one rooted in religious commitment, then there is no further justification that a scientist can offer for the primacy of scientific truth other than the fact that it is truth in terms of the standards and conventions of science.

There is also a further line of thought here. It is possible that science itself is not a unified entity. Maybe it manifests, or has manifested, a certain *internal* incommensurability. It is at this point that Thomas Kuhn, reluctant hero of the social constructivist Left, enters the picture.

In his book *The Structure of Scientific Revolutions*, Kuhn argues that what he calls 'normal science' takes place within the context of particular 'paradigms', which provide the rules and standards for scientific practice within any particular field of scientific enquiry. Paradigms are rooted in the agreement of scientific communities; they enable scientists to determine lines of enquiry, to formulate questions, to create appropriate research strategies, to interpret results, and to determine their relevance and meaning. It was Kuhn's view that a paradigm is essential to scientific enquiry: 'No natural history can be interpreted in the absence of at least some implicit body of intertwined theoretical and methodological belief that permits selection, evaluation, and criticism.'[31] George Ritzer expresses Kuhn's idea like this:

> A paradigm is a fundamental image of the subject matter within a science. It serves to define what should be studied, what questions should be asked, how they should be asked, and what rules should be followed in interpreting the answers obtained. The paradigm is the broadest unit of consensus within a science and serves to differentiate one scientific community (or subcommunity) from another.[32]

According to Kuhn, the history of science is marked by periodic 'scientific revolutions', each of which sees the prevailing paradigm in a particular field of enquiry overthrown by a new paradigm (as, for example, occurred when the Ptolemaic worldview was overthrown by the Copernican system). A scientific revolution is preceded by a period of 'crisis', during which time it is clear that an existing paradigm can no longer be sustained under the pressure of growing anomalies and puzzles. A revolution occurs when the scientific community shifts its allegiance to a new paradigm, at which point the crisis ends, and normal science resumes.

The interesting point for our purposes is that it is Kuhn's argument that paradigms can be radically incommensurate with each other. Indeed, he suggests that

> ... the proponents of competing paradigms practice their trades in different worlds ... In one, solutions are compounds, in the other mixtures ... Practicing in different worlds, the two groups of scientists see different things when they look from the same point in the same direction.[33]

To the extent that paradigms are incommensurate in this way, we're back to Winch's point about Western science and radically alien belief systems. If the rules, procedures and criteria for assessing truth-claims function only within paradigms – or forms of life – then it isn't possible to adjudicate between their competing claims. There is also no way to assess the relative merits of particular paradigms *in toto*, since there is no objective space, outside a paradigm, where such an assessment could take place or where its results might garner general agreement. It is very easy to see, then, how Kuhn's ideas have been seen as a form of epistemic relativism. Baghramian, for example, says that

> [the] relativistic implications of Kuhn's view seem evident. All assessments of the success, and even truth, of a particular scientific theory can be made only within and relative to a given paradigm – there is no room for extra-paradigmatic, non-relative evaluations in Kuhn's view of science.[34]

J.L. Austin once remarked that in the case of every important philosopher, 'there's the part where he says it, and the part where he takes it back'.[35] This is certainly true of Thomas Kuhn. He claimed not to be happy that many of his critics and supporters took him to be advocating a kind of anti-science relativism or irrationalism. Indeed, in the Postscript which first appeared in the second edition of *The Structure of Scientific Revolutions*, he seemed to retreat from the more radical stance of the earlier edition, arguing that 'Later scientific theories are better than earlier ones for solving puzzles in the often quite different environments to which they are applied. That is not a relativist's position, and it displays the sense in which I am a convinced believer in scientific progress.'[36]

It is also true that Kuhn had little time for radical, social con-structivist theories. Thus, John Horgan, in *The End of Science*, reports on a conversation he had with Stephen Jay Gould about Kuhn:

> I asked Gould if he believed, as Kuhn did, that science did not advance toward the truth. Shaking his head adamantly, Gould denied that Kuhn held such a position. 'I know him, obviously', Gould said. Although Kuhn was the 'intellectual father' of the social constructivists and relativists, he nonetheless believed that 'there's an objective world out there', Gould asserted; Kuhn felt that this objective world is in some sense very hard to define, but he certainly acknowledged that 'we have a better sense of what it is now than we did centuries ago'.[37]

And similarly, Kuhn himself has criticized what he saw as the excesses of the social constructivist position:

> Talk of evidence, or the rationality of claims drawn from it, and of the truth or probability of those claims has been seen as simply the rhetoric behind which the victorious party cloaks its power. What passes for scientific knowledge becomes, then, simply the belief of the winners. I am among those who have found the claims of the strong program absurd: an example of deconstruction gone mad.[38]

However, as we saw in the case of Wittgenstein, there is a sense in which all this is beside the point (though it is an interesting piece of intellectual history). Kuhn's ideas, whatever his intent, and even if he came to regret their original formulation, just did come to be associated with various kinds of anti-science radicalism; and his legacy, although he would not have chosen it, is as a standard-bearer for the social constructivists, radical anthropologists, postcolonialists and other postmodernists who for various reasons wish to challenge what they see as the hegemony of Western science.

Where does all this leave us?

The story which has unfolded here about scepticism, relativism and doubt could easily have featured a different cast of characters. It would have been just as pertinent to have talked about Kant's noumenal world; Nietzsche and perspectivism; Peirce's pragmatism; Derrida and deconstructionism; Foucault on power/knowledge; and Rorty's neopragmatism. But, in an important way, even with a different cast-list, the story would have been the same: it would have shown that philosophy is destined to be haunted by the possibility that we can never have absolute, foundational truth. But does it matter? John Dewey once remarked that old philosophical problems were never resolved; they simply stopped mattering.[39]

There is no doubt that many people find the kinds of ideas explored here, on first reflection at least, rather seductive; just maybe the army of sceptics and relativists has got it right, and there really is no knowable truth, or there are as many versions of it as there are forms of life. But further reflection should cast these ideas in a less persuasive light; partly for reasons to do with their logic, and in particular the thought we discussed earlier that both scepticism and relativism are self-defeating; but also for the reason, in many ways more interesting, that just about everybody already knows that they are false; and they know it in a visceral, primal, almost physical way that precedes reflection.

This latter claim is a strong one to make, so it is necessary to be absolutely clear about what is being asserted here. It is not that there are no beliefs which we hold with less than complete certainty. There are, of course, lots of beliefs like this; for example, we might believe that Saddam Hussein did (or did not) have weapons of mass destruction in 2003, but we can't be absolutely sure about it. This kind of ordinary doubt leads neither to scepticism nor to relativism. It is also not that there are no beliefs which have a fuzzy, may be true, may not be true, may be no answer to the question, kind of quality. As we'll suggest in a later chapter, people do have beliefs of this nature – perhaps, for example, about the existence of God. In this case, there is at least the threat of scepticism and relativism; if all our beliefs were fuzzy in this way, then it would suggest that we were naturally inclined towards certain sorts of philosophical doubt about truth. But not all of our beliefs are fuzzy in this way.

This leads to the question of precisely what *is* being asserted with the claim that just about everyone who is not psychotic already knows: that the ideas which motivate scepticism and relativism are false. It is being asserted variously that

- As we move through our daily lives, we very rarely question the epistemological status of those things we take to be more than just probably true: walls are solid; fire burns; knives cut; jumping off a cliff will cause serious injury; it hurts more to be hit with a rock than with a violet; rain is wet; heat cooks food; aeroplanes fly because engineers designed them according to various physical laws (not magic); there is no little gremlin inside a radio set; and so on.[40]

- We hold beliefs of this kind in a 'they are true all the way down to the bottom' sort of way. So for instance if a friend from another culture offers to apply a lighted match to our face, because in that other culture fire does not burn, we will not light up with smiles and eagerly accept. This is not because it *might* turn out after all that there are facts of the matter about fire and human skin, it is because we already know damn well that there are, and we know it all the way down.

- Beliefs that we think really certainly true, rather than just probably true, trump other fuzzy, may be true, may be false beliefs we hold. Thus, for example, the person who sort of believes that homeopathy might be true in a spiritual kind of way will choose standard, non-'alternative' painkillers for a third-degree burn.

- This all adds up to the fact that we know scepticism and relativism are false. Consider a thought-experiment to illustrate the point. An anthropologist has returned home after a year of field-work. She is walking down Gower Street absorbed in conversation with a shaman who, wanting to see the world, accompanied her to London. They are discussing the interesting fact the shaman has taught her, that large solid objects moving above a certain speed turn into a magical substance which conveys spiritual insight on contact and feels like expensive massage oil. The anthropologist, listening intently, steps off the pavement and the shaman does too; the anthropologist belatedly looks to her left and sees a bus almost on top of them; she leaps backward, yanking the shaman with her by the arm, as the bus roars over the spot where they had been, flattening a styrofoam burger box from McDonald's under its left front wheel. The anthropologist stands there with her mouth open, gazing at her baffled companion and wondering what on earth she is going to write in that article now.[41]

At this point, any remotely sophisticated philosopher will point out that the word 'know' is being used here to mean something like: *to believe with absolute certainty*; and they will further point out that this is not what philosophers tend to mean when they use the word, and that it is indisputable that people sometimes believe things with absolute certainty which they later come to believe were not true after all. And, of course, this is right; which is why an argument like the one being advanced here cannot rule out the *logical* possibility of scepticism and relativism.

However, there is a sense in which the philosophical response simply misses the point. The argument here is not that it isn't possible to doubt that there are facts of the matter about the world;

or that it isn't possible to think that truth is necessarily relative to cultures or forms of life. It is rather that we *don't* in fact do these things. Or, more precisely, the argument here is that our primary orientation to the world, the orientation in terms of which we *gear into* the world (to borrow some phenomenological terminology), will not allow us to doubt the fact that there are real, foundational truths about the world. This orientation is like the ratchet that makes elevators unable to fall: it makes it almost physically impossible for us to choose to override our visceral, instinctual certainty about real, foundational truths. This is shown variously by our fear of falling from great heights, our urge to jump out of the way of oncoming buses, and by our lack of inclination to put our hands into roaring fires. And, moreover, we are perfectly well aware of this even as we voice those philosophical arguments which deny it; we are aware of it in the fear we feel when we suddenly notice a car speeding towards us as we cross the street; in the sorrow or anger we feel when reading news of war crimes and tsunamis; in the thought we sometimes have in crowded shops or theatres – 'a hundred years from now every single person here will be dead'; and in the bitter recurrence of awareness of our own *certain* mortality.

The real puzzle, then, about the doctrines of scepticism and relativism is that nobody really believes them. Not in their bones.

3 The Truth Radicals

Neopragmatism, a postmodernist version of pragmatism which sees truth variously as, in the words of its best-known exponent, Richard Rorty, 'a rhetorical pat on the back' or 'whatever one's contemporaries let one get away with', began in the backwash of the political upheavals of the 1960s and 1970s. Morris Dickstein points out that the revival of pragmatism is a complicated phenomenon with a lot of crosscurrents; among them he cites a 'new impetus to radical thinking' in the 1960s, the shift of that impetus to the universities after the New Left collapsed, and the renewed disappointment with Marxism which caused apocalyptic thinking and 'the grand narratives of earlier systems' to go out of fashion, at which juncture the work of Rorty 'formed a bridge between a Deweyan faith in liberal democracy and a postmodern antifoundationalism'. If James's strong misreading of Peirce began pragmatism, Rorty's 'strong misreading of Dewey, whom he described as "a postmodernist before his time"', brought it to life again.[1]

Some ideas that originated in those upheavals and the manifestos they spawned are the progenitors of postmodernism. There was a much-remarked shift in the politics of that time from material bread-and-butter issues to issues of culture, attitude and thought. This was a natural outgrowth of the Civil Rights movement in the USA, as countless histories and memoirs of the period have attested. The process of battling inequality imposed on a group for transparently arbitrary reasons naturally does tend to stimulate people to wonder how such arbitrary injustices got a foothold in the first place. People are then likely to ask further questions, such as whether there are more such irrational injustices (and behold, there are many: treatment of and attitudes about women, gays, various nationalities and ethnic groups), and what it is about the way people think that results in such arrangements and allows them to be tolerated and ignored for so long. Thinking about questions like that, as everyone soon found, can cut very deep. It can suddenly seem that social arrangements and the thought-world that backs them up are riddled with holes, as if gnawed away by termites. The war in Algeria had a similar effect in France; the war in Vietnam drove the point home and made it global.[2]

Thus in the late 1960s and after, politics became ever more closely involved in culture: in examining and rethinking customs, habits, entrenched ideas and conventional wisdom. Gender roles, house-work, language: everything was up for grabs and subject to re-evaluation. And a good thing too. People who had been silent, submissive, marginal and ignored, took centre stage, and a great many casual injustices and barriers were done away with. This was an excellent thing – the results, and the rethinking process itself: both were an immense net benefit.

But there was some collateral damage, and postmodernism and epistemic relativism can be seen as examples.

The underlying idea in the rethinking process is that radical thought can go anywhere and tackle anything: that the rethinking is inherently and necessarily political, not factual or technical; that it is a matter of morals, of value, of justice, rather than one of statistics; of ought rather than is. This implies both that anyone and everyone is qualified to engage in it, and that no one is qualified to gainsay its insights on the basis of expertise or technical knowledge.

The scepticism about truth that we looked at in the previous chapter is very useful for this, and it plays a large role – as it always has when people want to deny or close the fact–value gap, when they want to ague that what we want to be true *is* true and no one can tell us it is not. In the sixteenth century scepticism was useful to enable religious conformity; in the late twentieth century it was useful to enable political, cultural and epistemic nonconformity (or rather 'nonconformity', since in its own world it was highly conformist).

And in fact the idea of conformity is more important to epistemic relativism than one might expect. There is often a note of bravado, rebellion and 'playfulness' in the assertions of standpoint epistemologists and postmodernists. Sandra Harding consistently refers to epistemology as 'conventional' epistemology in contrast to standpoint or feminist epistemology, thus framing standpoint epistemology as unconventional rather than potentially simply wrong. There is a strange idea lurking behind this framing: that epistemology is a matter of choice, and thus of fashion and convention, and of politics and commitment, as opposed to being a matter of truth or falsehood, warrant or the lack of it.

'Unconventional' epistemologists seem to view science itself as through and through conformist – not merely in obvious surface ways, such as being successful, well-paid, high-status, and so on, but in being tamely submissive to its own findings. In acquiescing to whatever the evidence may show, rather than being boldly Luciferian, hurling a despairing No even in the teeth of Yahweh himself.

This penchant for the defiant gesture, for proudly or 'playfully' denying reality, is a characteristic move of constructionist, postmodernist, standpoint and other radical theories. The translation of epistemic questions into political ones, and hence of errors and legless theories into political stances, is the rhetorical ploy that makes it work – 'work', that is, in the sense of persuading others.

This 'working' might seem counterproductive for the Left, given science's historical role as, in Daniel Dennett's phrase, the universal acid, the great solvent of tradition (since tradition so often boils down to traditions of who gets to oppress which groups). But there is a kind of logic to it, however flawed. This translation is, in the view of its practitioners, the logical outcome of projects to rethink everything. 'Everything' really does mean *everything*, the thinking goes, so positivists and conventional epistemologists who call a halt, who try to build walls and patrol borders around science, are selling out and giving up, surrendering to the most pervasive and oppressive power of all. Their scepticism of scepticism is not a cognitive or warranted or logical view but a regressive political failure: cowardice or venality or lack of imagination. Again, the matter is posed in moral and political terms rather than epistemic ones; translated, in short. Critics of standpoint epistemology are called conservative and reactionary, conventional and traditional, thus shifting the terms of the discussion from one of evidence, methodology, logic and accuracy, to one of basic morality. It is assumed (and sometimes explicitly said) that there is a moral imperative to press the interrogation of received wisdom all the way into science itself.

It is possible to tease out a kind of explanation for this view – an explanation of why it might make sense in moral and political terms even though it makes no sense in epistemic terms. Two concerns have always loomed large for the New or postmodern Left: liberation and egalitarianism. The rethinking projects have always had as a goal increasing liberation and doing away with hierarchies. Science cuts both ways in each endeavour. It is immensely liberating, but it is also confining: one is not free to choose the results one desires, or to change or conceal evidence. And it is both egalitarian and hierarchical: it is the career open to talents, so it is the very opposite of hierarchies based on birth, class, race or gender, but it is also the very essence of meritocracy, in that talent and hard work are required in order to do well, and there is such a thing as doing well. So because science does cut both ways, it is understandable that the Left is divided over these issues. Some of the Left adheres to Enlightenment ideas of rationality and empiricism, and some of it opts for what one might call paradigm-shift egalitarianism and liberation that goes past boundaries and stopping-points which used to be taken for granted. This brand of egalitarianism extends its reach into areas of life where it had not occurred to people to think it was relevant, Until Now.

The Until Now note is another that is struck often in postmodernist writing, a self-congratulatory 'only we have been bold and perceptive enough to see this' note. This aspect itself does a good deal to explain the roots and motivation of epistemic relativism. In that sense, the counter-intuitiveness, the perversity, the nonsensicality of many of the claims is in fact the point. The idea is that people simply failed to think of Startling Claim X before out of timidity or conformity, or awe of science and authority, or lack of imagination, or simply not being as shrewd and clever as the current generation; therefore the fact that the claim appears outlandish can be taken as merely more of the same timidity and failure of imagination. To the extent that this idea is in effect, it operates as an incentive to make outrageous claims, as opposed to a more usual scholarly incentive to temper such claims. Under the influence of this idea, the more outrageous the claim, the better.

Pre-paradigm-shift egalitarianism satisfied itself with legal and material equality, with doing away with unjust legal barriers, and so forth. Paradigm-shift egalitarianism wants to make more dramatic, far-reaching claims: claims that apply always and everywhere, that cannot be shut out as irrelevant or incompetent.

This radical egalitarianism applies not only to laws, pay-packets, school and university admissions policies, clubs and societies, but also to truth-claims and knowledge-claims, to disciplines, to knowledge itself.

And liberation is extended in a similar manner, beyond purely literal, material forms of liberty, into immaterial, almost metaphorical ones – though here there is less room for claims of novelty, since Rousseau, Blake, Marx, Emerson, Thoreau and Nietzsche, among others, provide ample precedent for ideas about liberating minds as well as bodies. Liberation from confining habits of thought as well as circumstances is the goal.

To both liberation and egalitarianism of this kind – concerned with mental chains and subtle forms of inequality – authority is seen as one of the chief opponents and obstacles of these more subtle, nuanced, covert, non-literal forms of imprisonment and inequality. Expertise tends to be associated with authority – tends in fact to be the basis of claims to authority, now that hierarchies of birth have lost much of their power. The most entrenched, respected form of expertise (leaving aside the celebrity-based forms belonging to athletes, rock stars, movie stars, TV news readers) is science. Therefore, science is the locus of the most powerful, influential, difficult-to-resist forms of expertise and authority, and hence hierarchy and power, in the contemporary world. Therefore its claims *must* be undermined and 'demystified'. Whether they are true or not is irrelevant; their harmfulness rests not on epistemic status but on their ability to compel assent and to exclude the ignorant.

Postmodernism and its various branches or cousins provide an array of tools, or subdisciplines, or Theories to effect this demystification. Standpoint epistemology is a way to 'problematize' universalism, and hence knowledge and science (which, if they are not true for all standpoints, are not really knowledge and science). Social constructivism argues that it is not only the rules of football and chess, traffic signals and money, that are the product of human manufacture, but also the natural world and the cosmos. Paul Forman, for example, wrote an influential article arguing that German physicists developed quantum mechanics out of a desire to salvage the prestige and status they had lost in the pessimistic Spenglerian mood of Weimar Germany. Cultural relativism argues that truth is truth, but only within a given paradigm or community (or, as we saw in the last chapter, language game or form of life). Feminist epistemology, in its more speculative incarnations, argues that because science has historically been a male preserve, therefore it is also likely to be warped by male bias, and thus needs to be rethought from the ground up.

Even if problematization and demystification can take some

eccentric forms, however, they can also do useful work; so we can do a little problematization and demystification of our own by taking a closer look at three thinkers in the postmodernist, social construct- ivist mould: Sandra Harding, Bruno Latour and Andrew Ross.

Sandra Harding

Sandra Harding is perhaps the best-known feminist epistemologist in the USA; her books *The Science Question in Feminism* and *Whose Science? Whose Knowledge?* are widely assigned in women's studies and even philosophy of science classes. In the latter book, Harding lists three main feminist tendencies toward generating new theories of knowledge: (1) feminist empiricism; (2) feminist standpoint theory; and (3) feminist postmodernism. Feminist empiricism is, Harding acknowledges, her own term for what its practitioners do not label at all: they simply think they are following the existing rules and principles of science with greater rigour. There are 'strengths and weaknesses' in feminist empiricism, Harding notes; she enumerates the strengths with some care. Many of the claims it puts forward, about biases in research and the like, are true, and thus feminist empiricism seems to leave much of scientists' and philosophers' 'conventional' understanding of the principles of properly conducted scientific research unchanged. Furthermore, the 'discourses of objectivity and truth/falsity are ancient and powerful. It is a great strength of feminist empiricism that it can enter and use these widely respected languages and conceptual schemes.' As a result, feminist empiricism is persuasive to natural and social scientists and to 'conventional' philosophers of science, and as Harding notes, other things such as 'distance of one's claims from falsity' being equal, persuasiveness is a good quality for an argument to have. This is especially true for women scientists who have entrenched hostility to deal with; it would be arrogant for philosophers to consider the justificatory strategies – such as making truthful claims – that allow feminists to continue their research mistaken or naïve. And one more conservative advantage of feminist empiricism is that 'it can be strengthened by appeal to "the ancients" – frequently a useful strategy in the face of disbelief'.[3]

But, all that conceded, feminist empiricism does not go far enough. 'The dominant conceptual schemes of the natural and social sciences fit the experience that Western men of the elite classes and races have of themselves and the world around them.'[4] Thus feminist standpoint epistemology has advantages over what Harding invariably calls 'conventional' epistemology.

Feminist critics of science argue that when one adds women as 'knowers' within 'traditional theories of knowledge', one finds how distorted and partial said theories actually are. The difficulty is that Harding's position commits her to the view that 'woman the knower' like 'woman scientist' seems to be a contradiction in terms. 'By "woman the knower" I mean women as agents of knowledge, as ... humans whose lives provide a grounding for knowledge claims that are different from and in some respects preferable to the knowledge claims grounded in the lives of men in the dominant groups.'[5] Harding explains the contradiction this way: to be scientific is to be dispassionate, impartial, disinterested, whereas to be a woman is to be emotional and interested in the wellbeing of friends and family. These differences are not the result of biology, but of various social conditions that apply to the lives of women more than they do to the lives of men in the dominant groups. Men assign to women the care of all bodies and of 'the local places where bodies exist'. The result is that men escape daily life in order to do the transcendent work of science, and the lives of women, embedded in daily life, are devalued.

> But from the perspective of groups that society excludes and margin-alizes, this now conventional claim that all knowers should be interchangeable can appear to have certain antidemocratic conse-quences. If all knowers are interchangeable, then affirmative action in the sciences can be 'only' a moral and political agenda. It can have no

possible positive consequences for the content or logic of the natural sciences; the scientific work of men and women, blacks and whites, Nazis and Ku Klux Klanners will be equally supervised and disciplined by scientific method. If all knowers are in principle interchangeable, then white, Western, economically privileged, heterosexual men can produce knowledge at least as good as anyone else can.[6]

Harding argues that the situations of men and women differ in many ways which offer useful resources for research, and that these differences can be seen as the grounds for feminist epistemology. Thus in Harding's view it is not the case that all knowers are, in principle, interchangeable. She cites eight such differences in particular:

- Knowledge of the world is supposed to be grounded in the world; human lives are part of that world; but men and women have different lives; therefore the fact that 'dominant knowledge claims' have been based largely in the lives of privileged men means that the resulting knowledge is incomplete. There are various ways of describing these differences. Jane Flax draws on object relations theory to analyse differences in male and female personality structure. Others, such as Carol Gilligan, Sara Ruddick, and Mary Belenky *et al.* cite different ways of reasoning that women develop to enable their different kinds of activity. But, Harding points out, there are difficulties in all this. There are 'many feminisms' and many views, not all of which can be right; so it is necessary to insist on an 'objective location' as the place to begin feminist research. That objective location is women's lives.
- Women are strangers to the social order. Their exclusion provides an advantage in the production of explanations of that social order.
- Because they are oppressed, women have less of a vested interest in ignorance about the social order. They are less likely to take the status quo at face value, thus their perspective reveals aspects of that social order that are difficult to see from the perspective of their oppressors' lives.

- Historians point out that history is written by the winners; thus because women are on the other side in the 'battle of the sexes', their perspective generates accounts of nature and social relations that are less distorted and partial.
- The perspective of women is from daily life, which is 'scientifically preferable' to a perspective from ruling activities. From the perspective of daily lives, conventional thinking can be seen to impede understanding of women's lives.
- Women's perspective is rooted in mediating the ideological dualism of nature versus culture. Nancy Hartsock puts it this way: 'The female experience of bearing and raising children involves a unity of mind and body more profound than is possible in the worker's instrumental activity.'[7]
- Women are outsiders.
- Now is the right time.

What to make of it?

There are many problems with all this, obviously enough. To name a few:

- Harding cites more than one oppressed category, and it is difficult to know how one would adjudicate among them. She refers to white, Western, economically privileged, heterosexual men as the standard for a privileged or dominant group, but things are of course not so clear-cut. To spell it out: not all straight white men are rich; not all rich men are white or straight; not all rich straight people are male or white, and so on. And by the same token not all women are poor, or non-white, or gay; not all non-white people are women, or poor, or gay; and so on again. How does one decide who is more privileged, who is more oppressed, among this smorgasbord of possible markers of either privilege or domination?
- Harding shifts without notice between claiming epistemic privilege for these somewhat confusing oppressed groups with

respect to the social world, and both the social and the natural worlds. It seems quite reasonable to think that experience of oppression or exclusion, poverty and difficulty, would be epistemically useful for knowledge of the social world; it seems quite another matter to think that such experience would make any productive or meaningful difference to one's research into and understanding of the natural world; of quantum mechanics or particle physics or microbiology.

- Harding fails to cite actual examples of how standpoint epistemology would in fact aid research into the natural world: she makes an a priori claim that it should, it can, it ought to, but she offers no evidence that it actually does.

- She offers little evidence for the corresponding claim that past research into the natural world has been distorted by the privileged position of the powerful men doing the research. She repeatedly cites Stephen Jay Gould's *Mismeasure of Man* and an article by Paul Forman, but one would expect more than two frequently recycled items to substantiate such large claims.

It is in a sense understandable that some feminists think of science as a male institution when so few women played a part in creating that institution, and since women were so thoroughly and firmly excluded during most of the time when the methodologies of science were being worked out. But the fact remains that there is nothing that can be done about that now. It is too late. Just as we cannot reach back in time to give Shakespeare's sister (and mother, wife, daughters) a grammar school education, so we cannot get science to start over again now. And if we could, there seems little reason to think the epistemology of science would be different. The subjects researched might be, but evaluation of evidence would not. Not unless feminists want to suppose that a larger mass of women in science would result in scientists' welcoming incompetence, mistakes, unwarranted claims, faked evidence, peer review replaced by mutual back-scratching; and one hopes that feminists do not want to suppose such a thing (though in Chapter 6 we see that some difference feminists risk supposing exactly that).

In fact, harsh though it may be to say it, Harding could be seen as a case in point herself – an object lesson in how epistemology is 'improved' by the addition of feminism. Her claims are so ill-founded and badly justified (as numerous critics have pointed out) that it is surprising they were ever published at all. Yet they were, and by Cornell University Press at that. And not only published, but on many a syllabus and cited in many a book, article and conference.

Bruno Latour

In their book, *Intellectual Impostures*, Alan Sokal and Jean Bricmont had this to say about Bruno Latour, the French sociologist who has made a name for himself in Science Studies: 'His works contain a great number of propositions formulated so ambiguously that they can hardly be taken literally. And when one removes the ambiguity … one reaches the conclusion that the assertion is either true but banal, or else surprising but manifestly false.'[8] Sokal and Bricmont's specific criticisms were directed mainly at Latour's book *Science in Action*; however, they might just as well have been directed towards *Pandora's Hope*, which was published some twelve years after *Science in Action*, because it is manifestly clear that Latour had changed very little in the intervening period.

Latour's style of writing in *Pandora's Hope* will be familiar to anyone who has dabbled in the kind of sociology which is inspired by writers in the 'Continental' tradition of philosophy. His prose, though not as impenetrable as that of the likes of Deleuze and Guattari, is peppered with neologisms and rhetorical flourishes. Thus, for example, he tells us that 'factishes'

> are types of action that do not fall into the comminatory choice between fact and belief. The neologism is a combination of facts and fetishes and

makes it obvious that the two have a common element of fabrication. Instead of opposing facts to fetishes, and instead of denouncing facts as fetishes, it is intended to take seriously the role of actors in all types of activities and thus to do away with the notion of belief.[9]

This kind of thing makes reading *Pandora's Hope* a frustrating experience, since one is never sure precisely what Latour means about anything. To the extent that it is possible to identify the book's central theme, it seems to be that in order to understand what science is up to, it is necessary to break down the 'old' subject–object dichotomy, which treats knowledge in terms of a fundamental division between knowing subjects and objects to be known. In its place, Latour wants to put something which looks a bit like – though presumably he would deny it – a souped-up version of Charles Sanders Peirce's pragmatism. Consider, for example, that he argues that 'Speaking truthfully about the world … is a very common practice for richly vascularised societies of bodies, instruments, scientists, and institutions. We speak truthfully because the world itself is articulated, not the other way around.'[10] The essence of his idea appears to be that the objects of scientific knowledge exist to the extent that they are articulated through the manifold mediations which constitute scientific practice. Roughly speaking, this means that scientists, objects, scientific equipment, extant scientific theory, modes of enquiry, institutional practices, and so on, are all part of a nexus which constitutes the objects of knowledge. Thus, for example, he argues that '"It refers to something there" indicates the safety, fluidity, traceability, and stability of a transverse series of aligned intermediaries, not an impossible correspondence between two far-apart vertical domains.'[11] For Latour, this kind of analysis has some radical implications. For example, he claims that existence is not an all-or-nothing property; rather, an entity gains in reality the more it is associated with other entities which in their turn collaborate with it.[12] And he insists that we should never say '"it exists" or "it does not exist"';[13] though it must be said that this is somewhat puzzling given that only a few pages earlier he had answered the question 'Did ferments exist before Pasteur made them up?' by saying: ' "No, they did not exist before he came along" – an answer that is obvious, natural, and even, as I will show, commonsensical!'[14]

It's hard to know what to make of all this. There is certainly a lot of conceptual muddying of the waters going on. Particularly, Latour likes to blur the distinction between our knowledge of objects and the objects themselves. Here are a few examples taken from his discussion of a paper by Louis Pasteur which deals with the discovery of a yeast related to lactic acid fermentation:

> The capacities of the natural world are modified between the beginning and the end of the story. At the start of the paper the reader lives in a world in which the relation between organic matter and ferments is that of contact and decay ... At the end the reader lives in a world in which a ferment is as active as any other already identified life form ...[15]

> It would be hard for something to have less existence than that! It is not an object but a cloud of transient perceptions ...[16]

> [H]ow can he increase the ontological status of this entity, how can he transform these fragile, uncertain boundaries into a sturdy envelope, how can he move from this 'name of action' to the 'name of a thing'?[17]

> It is possible to go from nonexistent entity to a generic class by passing through stages in which the entity is made of floating sense data, taken as a name of action, and then, finally turned into a plantlike and organised being with a place within a well-established taxonomy.[18]

It hardly needs pointing out that these statements are highly tendentious. If Latour is speaking metaphorically, then all this is just rhetoric, where the idea, surely, is to prepare the ground for the later argument he wants to make that the old dichotomy between subject and object, mind and nature, has been dissolved. If Latour is talking literally, then he assumes what he needs to demonstrate: namely, that the ontological status of objects, their nature, is affected by the process of coming to know about them.

This is not the first time that Latour has used this trick of translating statements about knowledge into statements about being. Sokal and Bricmont complained about precisely the same thing in *Intellectual Impostures*. Here is Latour's offending statement: 'Since the settlement of controversy is the *cause* of Nature's representation, not the consequence, we can never use the outcome – Nature – to explain how and why a controversy has been settled.'[19] This is what Sokal and Bricmont had to say about this piece of legerdemain:

> Note how Latour slips, without comment or argument, from 'Nature's representation' in the first half of this sentence to 'Nature' *tout court* in the second half. If we were to read 'Nature's representation' in *both* halves, then we'd have the truism that scientists' *representations* of Nature (that is, their theories) are arrived at by a social process, and that the course and outcome of that social process can't be explained simply by its outcomes.[20]

Perhaps the most striking thing about the work of Latour is just how much his arguments, whether intentionally or not, rely on rhetoric and misreading. For example, he cites Pasteur talking about the possibility of bias in research chemistry:

> Whenever a chemist makes a study of these mysterious phenomena and has the good fortune to bring about an important development, he will instinctively be *inclined* to assign their primary cause to a type of reaction *consistent* with the general results of his own research. It is the *logical* course of the human mind in all controversial questions.[21]

Latour then takes this statement to be indicative of Pasteur's commitment to two separate epistemologies; the one suggested above, which precludes 'impartial judgement'; and the orthodox, scientific epistemology, with its commitment to objectivity. But Pasteur's statement is indicative of no such thing. Nowhere does he suggest that truth-claims are *settled* by an appeal to personal inclination; nor does he claim that knowledge flows directly from the work of any *particular* scientist. Indeed, the whole point about scientific knowledge is that it is secured, tested and revised by the scientific community *as a whole*, precisely to neutralize the biases of individual scientists – a fact which Pasteur knows perfectly well: 'And it is my opinion, at this point in the development of my knowledge of the subject, that *whoever judges impartially* the results of this work and that which I shall *shortly publish* will recognise with me that fermentation appears to be correlative to life ...'[22]

Although Latour's rhetoric has a certain local effectiveness, its overall impact is to render him rather mute. The trouble is that it very quickly becomes clear that his arguments don't do the work that he claims for them, with the result that one begins to read his work from a default position of high suspicion. He does have interesting things to say about the genesis of scientific knowledge, but unfortunately only in the context of a shoddy epistemology, a dodgy grasp of logic and a fondness for the overblown turn of phrase.

Andrew Ross

Andrew Ross does not make a systematic argument, as he points out himself: the arguments he presents in *Strange Weather* are not based on the sort of 'close ethnographic study' that has been an exciting new approach in cultural studies.[23] The book, he says, is instead intended as a public discussion of issues about science and technology, not the definitive findings of a specialist. The style and approach are more like that of journalism or travel writing than of scholarly or philosophical analysis. Nevertheless he does make many broad statements about the truth-value and epistemic standing of science, rationality, empiricism, 'positivism', and so on. This combination – of a discursive, even conversational, style that makes no effort to back up its claims, with frequent strong claims about large subjects with technical underpinnings and broad implications – is a somewhat awkward one. When Ross tells us[24] that 'scientific rationality' is undergoing a 'legitimation crisis' and that many of the 'founding certitudes' of modern science have been 'demolished', we need more of an argument than mere mention of historically minded critics, feminists, ecologists and anthropologists along with Ross's claims that they have 'revealed' and 'exposed' something never specified. When he says that 'the empirical naming and knowing of the physical world is nothing if not a culturally expressive act with fully political meanings'[25] we wonder why we should accept such a statement. To put it another way: Ross makes a number of very strong claims, and offers very little in the way of evidence or argument for them.

Perhaps the reason this gap between the strong claims and the minuscule justification for them was allowed to pass is that Ross makes many of them by implication rather than explicitly. Rather than assert in so many words that science's authority and 'power', its position at the top of a putative hierarchy, is arbitrary and unjustifiable, he relies on what one might call innuendo by adjective. Science is associated with words such as authority, dominant, elitist, orthodox, while New Age is surrounded with words such as marginal, sublegitimate, community, contestatory.

The central claim of *Strange Weather* is that science does in fact function in the manner of other basically arbitrary hierarchies. Ross cites 'critics like Stanley Aronowitz' who 'see science not as the realisation of universal reason but simply as an ideology with a power that extends well beyond its own institutions' and then says we 'need a scientific culture that can learn from differences of class, gender, race, and biology, and that can transform notions like progress and objectivity in order to address these differences and the social inequalities created in their name'.[26] He then adds that it is beyond the scope of *Strange Weather* to 'detail the features' of such a culture; it is also apparently beyond its scope to 'detail' how such a thing is possible or coherent. It is difficult not to conclude that 'beyond the scope of this book' is simply a euphemism for disinclination or inability. Arguably, if it is beyond the scope of a given book to justify the implausible claims it makes, then it ought not to make them.

Ross draws an analogy between what he calls the 'demarcation lines' in science, and the boundaries between 'hierarchical taste cultures' – popular, middlebrow and high. In each, there are experts 'policing' the borders with their standards for exclusion and inclusion. Ross justifies this comparison on the grounds that, in the aftermath of Popper, falsifiability is often considered a criterion for 'scientific authenticity' despite the fact that such a criterion is no more 'objectively adequate' and no less mythical than for instance aesthetic complexity is in cultural criticism. He says the science–high culture analogy helps in understanding middlebrow aspects of New Age culture compared with highbrow scientific culture and lowbrow 'gadget fetishism' of popular science. Part of what it explains is the fact that New Age is, paradoxically, both alternative and deferential toward authority. The upshot is that intellectuals are happy to discuss and analyse soap operas, but they disdain New Age culture: those with cultural capital can afford to go slumming, but the middle has no appeal. Thus intellectuals need to create a more democratic cultural politics that would not be confined by this 'logic'.

Once the theoretical work is out of the way, much of *Strange Weather* is simply tourism, descriptive accounts of various odd beliefs and activities given a high theoretical gloss by way of speculative interpretations of those beliefs and activities. Ross suggests for instance that breakdowns in communication recounted by the 'channelling community' are necessary in 'narratives of contact' that would otherwise be too reminiscent of colonial narratives.[27] He moves from mention of the Heisenberg principle to the remark that the 'new "impossibility"': of physics' object of knowledge 'aligns' it with psychoanalysis and parapsychology, fields otherwise excluded from the 'scientifically constituted'.[28] He goes from a quite interesting discussion of notions of economy, streamlining, form follows function, ornament as waste in Bauhaus architecture, Ezra Pound's Imagism and the efficiency techniques of Taylorism, to the startling and unelaborated assertion that 'in recent years critics have come to see science itself as just another form of rhetoric'.[29]

Because of the nature of the material and the tone of the writing, it is hard to tell how literally all this is meant, how much of it is merely postmodern 'playfulness' and *jeu d'esprit*, punning and irony. Ross has a good deal of fun in the last chapter with a Foucauldian reading of the Weather Channel (a US cable channel that shows weather programming 24 hours a day), including the observation that anyone who watches the Weather Channel for the first time 'is surely left with an altered sense of how his or her body functions in a number of environments'. He ends with a rather vague connection of global warming and global citizenship.

Much of this may indeed be mere speculation and word-spinning in the traditional manner of English professors and belle lettrists, making Ross a sort of late-twentieth-century David Cecil – a description which would surely irritate him. But that is perhaps beside the point. It may all be layer upon layer of irony – but Ross does not in fact defend his work in such terms. Nor does he even consistently defend the principle that non-experts ought to be allowed and encouraged to give their opinions on subjects in which they are not experts. He had this to say in the aftermath of the 'Sokal Affair' at a forum on the subject at New York University in October 1996:

> It's reasonable to conclude that relatively few people actually read the issue [of *Social Text* in which Alan Sokal's article appeared], and yet there seemed very few who did not have a strong opinion about the Sokal affair, as it came to be known, and not a few who used the occasion to cast judgement on entire fields of scholarship, such as science studies and cultural studies, without showing much evidence of having read one word of the scholarship.[30]

It is impossible not to notice the irony of those last few words. It is not only that they belie Ross's oft-stated desire to create a 'more democratic cultural politics' and his disdain for cultural and taste 'hierarchies', for people, institutions, magazines and disciplines that are concerned with patrolling borders, exclusion and policing, in the sense of requiring evidence before taking claims seriously – though they certainly do. It is also that he himself shows no evidence at all of knowing anything whatever about the science he dismisses so casually and with so little in the way of what is normally considered 'scholarship'.

They also seem to make clear that Ross does not consider his work a mere game or extended joke, that he does consider it scholarship; therefore it should be addressed in such terms.

The basic claim of *Strange Weather* is that science's authority, status, prestige and position at the top of the knowledge hierarchy, and the political–cultural–rhetorical hierarchy as well, are both arbitrary and anti-democratic. 'How can metaphysical life theories and explanations taken seriously by millions be ignored or excluded by a small group of powerful people called "scientists"?'[31] This claim is not actually argued, as we have seen; it is merely asserted and reiterated throughout via rhetoric: science and rationality, realism and truth, are associated with the police, border-patrols, authority and other such categories. But Ross ignores the obviously crucial facts that (1) some authority is better justified than others, as are some forms of expertise, some exercises of control or power, and so on, and (2) there is a reason for the authority and prestige of science, a reason that goes beyond mere habits of deference. To put it bluntly, the reason is that the right answer has more authority than the wrong one. Ross neglects to address this rather important aspect of the question.

Science and other forms of empirical enquiry such as history and forensic investigation do have legitimate authority because the truth-claims they make are based on evidence (and are subject to change if new evidence is discovered). Other systems of ideas that make truth-claims that are not based on evidence, that rely instead on revelation, sacred books, dreams, visions, myths, subjective inner experience, and the like, lack legitimate authority because over many centuries it has gradually become understood that those are not reliable sources. They can be useful starting-points for theory-formation, as has often been pointed out. Theories can begin anywhere, even in dreams. But when it comes to justification, more reliable evidence is required. This is quite a large difference between science and pseudoscience, genuine enquiry and fake enquiry, but it is one that Ross does not take into account. The implication seems to be that for the sake of a 'more democratic culture' it is worth deciding that the wrong answer *ought* to have as much authority as the right one.

And yet of course it is unlikely that Ross really believes that. Surely if he did, he would not have written this book – he would not be able to claim that a more democratic culture is preferable to a less democratic one, or anything else that he claims in his work. However playful or quasi-ironic *Strange Weather* may be, it does lapse into seriousness at times, it does make claims that Ross clearly wants us to accept – because he thinks they are right as opposed to wrong. The intention of *Strange Weather* is to correct mistaken views of science and pseudoscience, to replace them with other, truer views. Ross cannot very well argue that his views are wrong and therefore we should believe them. He is in fact claiming authority for his own views, he is attempting to seek the higher part of a truth-hierarchy. The self-refuting problem we always see in epistemic relativism is here in its most obvious form.

And Ross ought to realize that if such claims *could* succeed they would eliminate all possibility for making the kinds of claims that the Left needs to make just as much as anyone else does. Truth-claims, evidence, reason, logic, warrant, are not some fiefdom or gated community or exclusive club. On the contrary. They are the property of everyone, and the only way to refute lies and mistakes. The Left has no more reason to want to live by lies and mistakes than anyone else has.

4 The Social Construction of Truth

One important, active – 'active' in the sense in which a volcano is active – 'site of contestation' in disputes over realism or relativism, truth or consequences, epistemology or politics, the warranted or the useful, is social constructivism in science and knowledge. The disagreement is between the claim that scientific knowledge is based on – and caused by – evidence, logic, rational inference, and the claim that it is based on and caused by social factors, interests, agendas (which are largely hidden or unacknowledged).

That is to put the issue in rather stark, unqualified terms, of course, and there are qualifications and details that can be added. Scientific realists acknowledge (in fact they insist) that scientific knowledge is always provisional, always subject to revision if better evidence is discovered, and most of them have no quarrel with the thought that social factors and extraneous agendas can shape priorities, lines of enquiry, funding, education, and the like. And some constructivists (though, surprisingly, not all) accept that evidence and logic play some part in the creation of scientific knowledge, and simply give social factors a more or less large role in addition to rational ones.

But not all, and that's where the volcano begins to rumble and heave. Some constructivists, via a combination of radical scepticism and Marxoforensic *cuibono*ism, claim that scientific theories are indeed chosen and institutionalized by way of anything and everything except good evidence: by class interest, status anxiety, desire for prestige, and the like.

The common ground between the two, the generally undisputed idea that social pressures and interests can shape and influence institutional factors, lines of enquiry, funding, and so on, was the uncontroversial subject matter of sociology of science until the 1970s. It is often called Mertonian sociology of science after its best-known and most influential originator and practitioner, Robert Merton. It is also often called the 'weak programme' in SSK – sociology of science and knowledge – particularly by practitioners and partisans of the 'strong programme' who, as the names flag up clearly enough, conceive of themselves as improving, expanding, correcting and overturning the Mertonian programme.

The thought is that Mertonian sociology of science doesn't go far enough, that it leaves much of the subject unexplored and unexplained, that it stops short in an arbitrary, deferential, timid and unscientific fashion. The philosopher of science David Bloor, in his *Knowledge and Social Imagery*, treats this stopping-short, this boundary-drawing, as a sort of taboo. He compares the distinction that Mertonian sociology makes between what sociology can and should explain and what it can and should not – between context and content – to Durkheim's categories of sacred and profane. The weak programme declares itself unable to explain the *content* of scientific knowledge as if that subject were an inner sanctum or holy of holies – which is an anti-scientific belief about science. Bloor says that this amounts to science exempting itself, alone among subjects, from scientific explanation.

> Can the sociology of knowledge investigate and explain the very content and nature of scientific knowledge? Many sociologists believe that it cannot. They say that knowledge as such, as distinct from the circumstances surrounding its production, is beyond their grasp. They voluntarily limit the scope of their own enquiries. I shall argue that this is a betrayal of their disciplinary standpoint. All knowledge, whether it be in the empirical sciences or even in mathematics, should be treated, through and through, as material for investigation ... There are no limitations which lie in the absolute or transcendent character of scientific

knowledge itself, or in the special nature of rationality, validity, truth or objectivity.[1]

If it is true that scientific knowledge itself cannot be investigated scientifically, Bloor says, then there is a paradox and a problem at the centre of science.

> Suppose that some of the detailed objections to the sociology of scientific knowledge had proved insurmountable, what would this have meant? It would have meant that there was a most striking oddity and irony at the very heart of our culture. If sociology could not be applied in a thoroughgoing way to scientific knowledge it would mean that science could not scientifically know itself.[2]

Science must be subject to naturalistic explanation – because what other kind is there? As James Robert Brown puts it:

> Naturalists are motivated by the thought that the natural world is all that there is and the scientific approach is the only way to comprehend it. There is no god, nor any corresponding religious understanding of the world ... All knowledge is scientific knowledge – there is no other kind. We must, says the naturalist, understand all our activities wholly in natural terms, and this includes the activity of science itself. Neither god nor platonic forms, nor anything else that is in any way mysterious or unnatural plays a part in our genuine knowledge.[3]

David Bloor, along with the sociologist Barry Barnes, two of the founders of what is known as the Edinburgh school of SSK, created the strong programme. Bloor's *Knowledge and Social Imagery* is one of the most important and influential documents of that programme. In it Bloor explains that sociologists, as good scientists, want to give a naturalistic account of knowledge, and that this entails looking for the causes of all beliefs (true as well as false) impartially, from a non-evaluative standpoint. Non-evaluative means, in this context, not separating 'good' or true beliefs from 'bad' or false ones and investigating only the latter, but rather considering all as the same sort of phenomenon and all as equally problematic and in need of causal explanation.

Bloor argues that there is a fundamental opposition between traditional rationalist accounts and naturalistic accounts. The only alternative to a naturalistic explanation, he says, is a teleological one: i.e. one that illegitimately (illegitimately from a naturalist perspective) derives explanation from purpose. Naturalistic explanations cannot take the form 'X exists or functions as it does because its purpose is Y', because naturalistic explanations cannot presuppose conscious, planned, intentional forces such as purpose. It explains nothing – and it isn't true – to say 'it rained because the crops needed water'. Bloor's argument is that traditionalist accounts of scientific beliefs are teleological in this way: they assert something like 'scientists accept belief X, because it is supported by evidence Y.'

Against the traditionalist account, he argues that, as is well known, theories are underdetermined by data. The fact that there are many different possible theories to explain the data, the fact that the data never force acceptance of any particular theory, means that there can be (or should be, or must be) explanations other than data for why theories become accepted. One of these explanations, one cause, may be (or, on some accounts, must be) 'interests'.

Bloor points out that categories and classifications are not in nature, not 'there' to be found, but created by humans. They vary between cultures, and the makers of categories can always choose different features to treat as salient. (The linguist George Lakoff makes a similar point from a different angle in *Women, Fire, and Dangerous Things*.) Thus biological taxonomy, for example, is not simply a transparent account of that which exists but a socially agreed system for organizing and thinking about what exists. In a similar way, Bloor points out that scientific observation in fact consists not of observation but of reports of observation.

The observation itself is always mediated, always translated into words, writing, tables, and therefore always social.

Haack, Brown, Kitcher

Different philosophers of science carve the subject up in different ways. Susan Haack talks of sober and inebriated SSK, and of Old Deferentialists and New Cynics. James R. Brown divides social construction of science into a nihilist wing and a naturalist one. Philip Kitcher identifies two clusters of ideas, the realist–rationalist, in which:

- Most scientific research is progressive, which results in increased ability to predict and intervene.
- This increased ability to predict and intervene allows us to claim that entities of the sort described in scientific research exist independently of our theorizing about them and that many of our descriptions are largely correct.
- All the same, our claims are vulnerable to future refutation. We may claim that our representations of nature are largely correct while still acknowledging that we may have to revise them tomorrow.
- Typically our views in the most prominent areas of science are based on evidence, and disputes are settled by appeal to canons of reason and evidence.
- Those canons of reason and evidence also progress as we discover more about the world and also more about how to find out about the world.[4]

And the social–historical, in which

- Science is done by human beings, which means by cognitively limited beings who live in complex social groups with long histories.
- Scientists all arrive at the laboratory or the field with preconceptions that have been shaped by the prior history of the groups they belong to.
- The social structures of science affect the ways research is

communicated and received, and this can have an impact on
debates among theories.

● The social structures in which science is embedded affect the
kinds of questions that are considered important and, sometimes,
the answers that are proposed and accepted.[5]

Kitcher points out that the best philosophy, history and sociology of
science (such as Martin Rudwick's *The Great Devonian Controversy*)
does full justice to both. Philosophy and social study of science go
wrong if they neglect one or the other.

Susan Haack makes a similar point in *Defending Science – Within
Reason*:

> Scientific evidence is usually the shared resource of a whole sub-
> community; enquiry in the sciences, cooperative or competitive, involves
> many people ... and science is not conducted in a vacuum, but in a larger
> social setting which may exert a significant influence on what questions
> get investigated, what research gets funded, what results get a wide
> audience – and sometimes on what conclusions get reached ... [S]tudies
> of the internal organisation of science and its external environment can
> help us discern what encourages, and what discourages, good, honest,
> thorough enquiry, free and accessible availability of results, etc. – a
> potentially very fruitful cooperation of sociology of science with
> epistemology.[6]

That, Haack says, is what she has in mind when she talks about 'the
sensible program' in sociology of science. The problem with the
inebriated or nihilist variety of sociology of science and knowledge is
that it focuses on everything *except* epistemic issues. Thus James
Robert Brown notes that Barnes and Bloor say they are interested in
'causes as "evidencing reasons"' and asks what they mean, and what
this has to do with contexts. He points out that the examples of
'contexts' that Barnes and Bloor give are all political: they include
background assumptions and beliefs that smack of social interests
rather than scientific beliefs.

Thus, the context in which Pouchet is considered is the politically and religiously conservative France of the mid-nineteenth century. This, however, is the social context. The epistemic context – the context that matters when it comes to reasons – is ignored. This latter context would include background assumptions from chemistry, biology, and so on. It is the 'scientific' assumptions that play the relevant causal role in a so-called rational explanation of belief and belief change … It is the *scientific*, not the social context, that one must appeal to in using contextualized reason-explanations. This is what Barnes and Bloor fail to do.[7]

Why is that?

Why?

Here we all are, in a sort of endless line dance, or snake swallowing tail, trying to explain each other. Why do those people believe what they do?, we all ask. Why do they think, say, write what they do? Let us look into the matter – let us investigate and try to explain what causes such beliefs, thoughts, opinions and ideas. What motivates people to form them, accept them and defend them?

It's tricky work, trying to understand and explain motivation. The potential for error is vast; the possibility of certainty is non-existent. Other minds are other minds, and what is going on in them is known only to the occupants – and often not even to them. But then, motivation is the very subject matter of SSK, of the Strong Programme, and of social constructivism in general. The question 'why do those people believe what they do?' is exactly the question all of them ask. So naturally everyone else can ask 'why do social constructivists believe what they do?'

It's a speculative, a priori, armchair sort of activity, of course, trying to decipher other people's motivations. It's a Sherlock Holmes in the sitting room of 221B Baker Street as opposed to in the field sort of enquiry, a three-pipe problem as opposed to an examination of marks on a windowsill or a perusal of someone's overcoat. Guesswork, in short. But it's a useful, necessary, productive form of enquiry for all that, particularly as an opening manoeuvre. Such hypotheses may not be checkable at all, in which case they remain highly speculative and tentative, hedged about with question-marks and perhapses. But the questions still need to be asked. The enquiry is speculative and upholstery-bound, but not daft. It's an old question: *cui bono* – and a massively important one. It's a major branch of the old philosophical distinction between appearance and reality, and the one at the heart of unmasking, demystifying, deconstructing, and so correcting many forms of human exploitation, oppression and injustice. *Cui bono*: in whose interest is it to declare that this or that group of people is inferior, subordinate, and thus suited and destined to toil for others? In whose interest is it to declare that this or that commodity is harmless, useful, healthy, redolent of sex, essential to happiness?

Of course the questions have to be asked. People are always going to *say* their reasons and motives are benign, public-spirited, respectable and admirable. Well they would, wouldn't they? as Mandy Rice-Davies so incisively put it. It's always reasonable to ask: SSK can ask, and so can we.

So why do they? Many reasons, it seems, epistemic as well as social, political as well as cultural. Social constructivism is in the air, it's part of the *Zeitgeist*, it's what we all grew up on. It simply seems right, natural, self-evident. It seems explanatory. It's satisfying, in an intellectual way, because it seems to make sense of things. It seems to fit. In short, it provides the usual motivation to believe something: it seems plausible.

- It is, or is thought to be, politically useful. The nature/convention distinction has always been used by and associated with the forces of progress and change, from at least the days of the Sophists, and probably far longer than that. The reasons are obvious enough: if a particular practice is indeed conventional rather than natural, that means humans have at some point chosen it, so they are at liberty to unchoose it again. It is the conservative, let's stick to the status quo party that has an interest in declaring favoured practices to be natural and therefore unalterable (unalterable without strain, damage, likelihood of disaster). The novelty, to the extent that there is novelty, lies in extending the distinction to epistemology. Supporters of rational enquiry generally tend to think social constructivism works very well when analysing kinship, taboos, religion, social practices, and the like, but not when analysing the warranted findings of scientific research.

- Thoroughness and completeness. Social constructivists say that it is arbitrary, or cowardly, or weak, or a betrayal, and the like, to stop short with social construction of other customs and not include knowledge. The thinking is that if social constructivism works anywhere in analysing human endeavours – and it manifestly does work – then surely it must work everywhere. Humans are always and everywhere humans, their customs and practices are human customs and practices, so there is always at least the possibility that those practices are created, voluntary, decided on: social. Thoroughness and completeness are generally seen as virtues in rational empirical enquiry, so surely they are virtues here.

- It can enable an attractively modest, non-domineering, anti-colonialist, anti-ethnocentric account of knowledge, or know-ledges. Scientific knowledge (seen in this account as 'Western', which is sharply contested by non-Western scientists, who are not few in number) is on this view not 'naturally' superior or even more functional than other 'knowledges', it is simply the local custom. It is no more (and in fact and practice possibly less) deserving of respect and entitled to authority than any other local knowledge. Thus the burden of empire is laid down.

- It is seen as anti-authoritarian. Science is often viewed as a source of (illegitimate) power and authority, and authority of a peculiarly unassailable kind, because based or rooted in detailed expert knowledge that the vast majority of people simply have no idea how to contradict or evaluate. This is rightly seen as a situation fraught with dangers. So, the more science can be portrayed and understood as a matter of convention and interests rather than well-warranted knowledge, the more possibility there is to keep its power in check.

- Similarly, science is seen as undemocratic, elitist, hierarchical, meritocratic, and ruthless: the very model of an anti-egalitarian status-conscious ambitious world. These qualities are, at least, regarded with ambivalence by much of the Left, and for good reason – they may be of utilitarian and instrumental value but they also (at least potentially) foster attitudes, values, and human relations that are problematic. To put it simply, they tend to produce winners and losers, and the attitudes and manners that go with that, and there is much to regret in that production. So, again, if scientific knowledge can be portrayed as less rationally based than had been thought, perhaps some of its inegalitarian aspects can be smoothed away.

- Historically at various times science has tended to exclude women, minorities, the poor – marginalized people in general. People who had access to elite education have had an enormous head-start in scientific careers, and those people have tended (and still tend) to be white males. In this sense, science has always been and still is (though less so to the extent that public education has improved) a privileged enclave, and one whose privilege has much to do with an accident of birth. Social constructivism is seen as one way to redress the balance, by improving science's representativeness.

- Science is seen as inimical to whole aspects of life that are of great importance to many people: the religious or 'spiritual', the imaginative, the aesthetic, the moral, and even to some extent the affective and emotional. Social constructivism functions as a sort of ally in the struggle to clip science's wings, to curb its perceived arrogance, to forbid it to second-guess people about their cherished deities or angels or alternative medications.

- Science is seen as just plain dangerous – in part for good reason. Science comes up with new medicines and computer software, yes, but it also comes up with new weapons and surveillance techniques.
- Science spoils the mystery. It unweaves the rainbow, it offers a single vision. It pokes in everywhere, it explains everything, and it rudely tells us we're hallucinating. We prefer poetry and *The X-Files*. If science is just another language-game or system of representation, perhaps we can keep them, without feeling infantile or silly.
- There is the appeal of radicalism itself; the appeal of pushing ideas as far as they can go, if not farther. The appeal of being outrageous, of frightening the horses, of making claims that prompt dull stuffy literal people (like scientists and 'positivists') to get indignant.
- There is the Don't Fence Me In aspect. The suspicion and problematization of *all* boundaries, borders, demarcations, distinctions, binary oppositions, as a form of social control, policing, territorial scent-marking. Hence the traditional or 'conventional' thought that some forms of knowledge are socially constructed, while others are not, is another instance of fencing the commons. By what right does science declare itself special or exempt or somehow outside and different from ordinary human activity?
- There is a disciplinary motivation – because natural science tends to dominate social science and the humanities, in the sense of getting both more respect and more money.
- There is a vocational motivation: strong social constructivism provides something new to say, hence publication, attention, enrolments, promotion, tenure, conference invitations, and the like.
- At least at the level of thought-experiment, there is some basic plausibility to the idea – especially for people who don't actually know any science from the inside, who aren't familiar with how

copious and detailed empirical evidence can be. It is always possible at least to imagine that All is Illusion, that the evil demon has us fooled, that our senses are systematically unreliable and that our idea of how things are is nothing like the way things really are. The basic sceptical position, in other words, cannot be disproved. So social constructivism could be true.

Scepticism all the way down

Here we come back to the sceptical impasse we saw in Chapter 2. The radically sceptical position may be true; the evil demon may be tricking us; there is no way to disprove the possibility. But then that possibility applies across the board. It's no good saying 'You're a brain in a vat and I'm not', because it could just as well be the other way around. By the same token it's no good saying 'You're delusional about evidence and the truth-claims you think your evidence warrants, but I'm right about my evidence and the truth-claims I think it warrants.' Why would that be the case? Why is your view privileged?

Philip Kitcher puts it this way:

> If the invitation is to throw away all our beliefs, start from scratch, and justify the claim that the objects about which we form perceptual beliefs are as we represent them, then we could not offer our contemporary blend of physics, physiology, and psychology to advance the kind of picture of perception I have sketched. But neither can champions of Science Studies offer any rival picture, even one that uses screens, veils, or cave walls. Descartes launched philosophy on a quest for fundamental justification, and despite the many insights uncovered by him and his brilliant successors, we now know that the problem he posed is insoluble … If the constructivist reminds us that we haven't shown on the basis of a set of principles that precede the deliverance of empirical science that our scientific opinions are reliable, the right response is to confess that we haven't. There is no such set of principles that will do that job, but by the same token, no set of principles will establish a constructivist picture.[8]

So, since SSK is saying something – since Sociology of Science and Knowledge is by definition saying something about science and knowledge, since saying something about science and knowledge is coterminous with the discipline – we can take it that the radical sceptical position is not the issue here. We can proceed on the assumption that, for the purposes of this discussion, we all think, and we all act as if we think, that we can find something out, however provisional and tentative it may be. We are all, equally, engaged in trying to discover a truth of the matter.

SSK and the Strong Programme are trying to find a truth of the matter – a true answer to the question – of what causes belief? And in particular, what causes scientific belief? It is not taking a Pyrrhonist position on the question. It is not saying that there is no truth of the matter, no true answer to the question; it is not even making the more limited claim that whether or not there is a truth of the matter, we mere mortals, or we mere sociologists and philosophers of science, are not equipped to find it out. On the contrary, they are making several quite robust claims that go in the opposite direction: that there is a truth of the matter, that it is different from the commonly accepted conventional wisdom on the subject, that they have found it out, and that they are going to communicate this truth to the world, and correct the distorted, incomplete, incorrect, illusion-fostering view of the matter that has prevailed until now. None of this has much to do with thorough-going scepticism.

In fact one could argue that the whole enterprise is motivated by and founded on a heightened dedication to ferreting out the truth, to separating appearance from reality, folk epistemology from how things actually are. People who are genuinely indifferent to truth, who are content to muddle along with whatever understanding of the world 'works' for some purpose or other, or makes them feel cheerful and comforted, don't undertake such endeavours.

They have no reason to; the questions don't catch hold of them. It's people who are always wondering what's *really* going on behind what seems to be going on, who saddle up such Rocinantes and ride away towards the windmills.

And they do useful work. There is widespread agreement that what Susan Haack calls the Old Deferentialist picture of science was indeed flawed – incomplete, impoverished, dull, and above all misleading. Martin Rudwick comments on this in *The Great Devonian Controversy*:

> Some philosophers may continue to portray natural science as 'a ship of reason powering its own way through a silent sea of social contingencies'. Those who are concerned with what scientists really did in the past – or with what they do at present – have rightly rejected that image as incompatible with any truthful description of scientific activity.[9]

But in seeking to correct the deferential picture they overshoot the mark – as Rudwick goes on to say:

> But some have now swung to the opposite extreme, presenting science as the making of model ships in bottles with an entirely questionable relation to any real ships there may be in the world outside. But if scientific activity is in any sense a social 'learning machine', by which human beings can gain some kind of reliable knowledge of the natural world, then the question of external reference cannot be shelved or evaded.[10]

So again we come to the why question.

One answer, as we've seen, is that social constructivists want a naturalistic explanation. Scientists are engaged in the attempt to explain nature, and are also themselves a part of nature. So their attempts to explain nature also have a scientific, which is to say, a materialist, naturalistic explanation, and so do their beliefs, results, theories, explanations: their knowledge. Their beliefs, theories and knowledge are not special or exempt in some way, not transcendent, not outside nature, as Bloor points out in *Knowledge and Social Imagery*. Explanation is explanation is explanation. It is not legitimate to have one kind of explanation for, say, animal locomotion, and another for scientific reasoning. Both are necessarily physical processes (they cannot be non-physical, after all – scientific reasoning cannot proceed without scientists' brains to carry it out), thus both have physical, naturalistic causes.

In one sense – a rather abstract, thought-experiment-like sense – one can see considerable point to this idea. Beliefs must have causes, and the causes must be part of nature, so a naturalistic explanation must be right. Perhaps it is merely a self-flattering illusion that scientific beliefs are caused by scientists' acceptance of evidence and logic; maybe they are caused by stomach pains or atmospheric pressure instead. Maybe explanations that cite evidence and reason are *post facto* constructions, like the stories we construct from dreams to make narratives out of random synaptic firings.

One could attempt to explain scientific beliefs on analogy with explaining digestion or coughing, as purely material, physical, observable, quantifiable, and the like. Such a method may lay bare habits, assumptions, preconceptions, observation-shaping theories, and so on. But it also seems doomed to produce a distorted picture, especially if the ethnographic or behaviourist perspective is maintained to the end. One may simply define scientific belief, and what one wants to discover about it, as a purely physical, reflex act, a bit of behaviour, externally visible but with no intentionality – but then one won't find out much about the questions SSK is asking.

Or there is the anthropological or ethnographic approach. Again, one might elect to do this as a form of abstraction, defamiliarization, of making it strange, in Brecht's phrase, as Garfinkel did with his ethnomethodology. Indeed, this is one approach to analysis of science, as Martin Rudwick points out:

> Some [analysts of science] have studied scientific research by being accepted as participant-observers within a laboratory. They have used the perspective and even the techniques of the anthropologist, treating the scientists as exotic natives with strange and puzzling customs. These ethnographers or microsociologists have given some detailed and illuminating accounts of routine procedures in scientific research.[11]

But, again, the defamiliarizing thought-experiment is at least as much of a limitation as a source of fresh insights.

> But ... they often show an extreme scepticism – or at least an extreme agnosticism – about the status of the knowledge the scientists claim to be producing. In minimizing if not discounting its reference to any 'real' external world of nature, their accounts of science open up a gulf of understanding between themselves and the scientists they observe – a gulf which surely no modern anthropologist would find tolerable in the interpretation of exotic cultures.[12]

What are interests?

The problem may be partly a matter of definition. For instance, the claim that one of the reasons or causes for scientific belief is 'interests', is more or less convincing depending on how 'interest' is defined. The implication is that class, status, power, money interests are the only salient kind. But those are not the only 'interests'. Enquirers also often have an interest in understanding, in getting things right, in getting at the truth, in seeing things as they really are in themselves. It may at a time be the case that class interest trumps epistemic interest – but it may equally be the case that the reverse is true. Human motivation is notoriously complex, various, opaque, contradictory, pulling in many directions at once. And scientists and enquirers are equally notoriously an unworldly, peculiar bunch, with motivations that differ from those of 'most people' – that's why they are called geeks and nerds. So it's surely just as likely to be misleading to assume that social and class interests always defeat epistemic ones as it is to assume the reverse.

But perhaps social causes, contexts and interests seem genuinely more plausible as causal explanations for beliefs than do their epistemic equivalents. Perhaps it seems that social and political interests can make things happen, while epistemic and scientific interests cannot. Perhaps social and political interests are seen as robust, powerful and active, while epistemic and scientific interests are seen as weak and inert.

Perhaps there is an assumption – a background theory of the kind that SSK likes to remind us always shapes observation – that social contexts and interests are natural, and so properly part of a 'naturalistic' explanation, in a way that epistemic and scientific interests are not. The Strong Programme stipulates that a naturalistic explanation is required; perhaps Strong Programmers see social interests as more material, more physicalist, and thus more powerful, more part of the real world, than purely (or merely) mental entities like epistemic and scientific interests. Could it be that epistemic and scientific interests are viewed, on an analogy with materialist views of consciousness, as epiphenomena? As subjectively felt, but powerless to make anything happen – mere whistles on the engine? Maybe to sociologists of knowledge, realists are simply embedded in a dream-world of mentalese, unable to pierce the veil of illusion surrounding consciousness, unphilosophically taking the appearance for the reality.

There is a great deal of 'perhaps' and 'could' in all this, but that seems inevitable in the nature of the subject. Causality is a notoriously difficult thing to explain, and minds are another: therefore explaining the causality of beliefs has to be at least doubly tricky, and perhaps exponentially so. Causality is often deeply hidden. We may think we have found it, but we can seldom if ever be sure we have. And minds are just as occult. One can remove a piece of skull, insert probes, look at PET scans, one can peer at the damp grey walnut all one likes, and one will not be able to watch a belief forming. Thus determining the causes of particular beliefs has to be an enterprise riddled with guesswork and uncertainty, and with immense possibilities for getting it wrong. And not only getting it wrong, but getting it wrong without any way to know you've got it wrong.

Philip Kitcher describes the situation this way:

Many critics of Science Studies recognise the relativism that often runs rampant ... [The] road to relativism is paved with the best of intentions and the worst of arguments. So practitioners come to inscribe on their hearts the Four Dogmas: (1) There is no truth save social acceptance; (2) no system of belief is constrained by reason or reality, and no system of belief is privileged; (3) there shall be no asymmetries in explanation of truth or falsehood, society or nature; and (4) honour must always be given to the 'actors' categories' ... When the Four Dogmas have been thoroughly absorbed, so that younger scholars start from their conclusions as if they were gospel, then enterprises of real peculiarity can be launched.[13]

And he adds an amusing but alarming footnote:

Anyone who has tried to talk to people who have recently been trained in Science Studies will know that the conclusions of the four arguments I have criticised are treated as axiomatic. There is just no questioning them, and one's raising of questions reveals that one must be a strange relic of the unenlightened past.[14]

An important prop for the second of the Four Dogmas is the theory-ladenness of observation. It is hard not to notice that it seems to be that very theory-ladenness which causes social constructivists to see social 'interests', not in addition to epistemic ones but instead of them. Martin Rudwick includes a cartoon from 1831 in *The Great Devonian Controversy*. It shows a gentleman in gentlemanly dress, probably Charles Lyell, standing on ground labelled 'Theory' and handing a pair of tinted spectacles to a dressed-for-fieldwork geologist carrying a collecting sack. Look through the tinted spectacles of Theory and get a tinted idea of what you're observing, is the clear implication. It seems that social constructivists look through their own theory-spectacles, and see social interests expand to blot out the landscape, and epistemic interests shrink into invisibility.

5   Politics, Ideology and Evolutionary Biology

Although science has enjoyed unparalleled success in helping us to find out about the world, it would not be true to think that things never go wrong with the scientific process. It is easy, for example, to find instances where political and ideological commitments have infected the truth-claims which have been made in the name of science. Lysenkoism is perhaps the best example of this pheno-menon. Trofim Lysenko, a Soviet agronomist, and his colleagues, in the name of dialectical materialism, were committed to a kind of pseudoscientific Lamarckism (the idea that it is possible for an organism to inherit acquired characteristics); and, with a view to expunging 'bourgeois science' from Soviet society, in the middle part of the twentieth century, they variously: persecuted their Mendelian opponents; destroyed books; eradicated all stocks of *Drosophila*; and embarked on agricultural policies which proved disastrous for the Soviet agricultural economy.[1]

However, it is an interesting facet of Lysenkoism, and one rarely commented upon, that there were elements of truth in the criticisms which it made of Western evolutionary thought. Not, of course, on the science side of things; Lamarckism proper was dead and buried as a live possibility some time before Lysenkoism ever really got going. But there was something to the criticism it made that Darwinist ideas had been taken in some unpleasant directions in the West. For example, in 1947 Lysenko argued that

All mankind belongs to one biological species. Hence, bourgeois science had to invent intraspecific struggle. In nature, they say, within each species there is a cruel struggle for food, which is in short supply, and for living conditions. The stronger, better adapted individuals are the victors. The same, then, occurs among people: the capitalists have millions, the workers live in poverty, because the capitalists supposedly are more intelligent and more able because of their heredity ... By means of the fabricated intraspecific competition, 'the eternal laws of nature', they are attempting to justify the class struggle and the oppression, by white Americans, of Negroes.[2]

Although intraspecific competition is not a fantasy, it is nevertheless true that the concept has been invoked in order to support a *laissez-faire* attitude towards the inequalities associated with unfettered capitalism. For example, Herbert Spencer, the chief exponent of social Darwinism, argued that those who favoured intervening to help the poorest members of society were 'blind to the fact, that under the natural order of things, society is constantly excreting its unhealthy, imbecile, slow, vacillating, faithless members';[3] and that 'If the unworthy are helped to increase, by shielding them from that mortality which their unworthiness would naturally entail, the effect is to produce, generation after generation, a greater unworthiness'.[4] Even Darwin flirted with this kind of thinking. Particularly, he worried about the effects on society of the fact that human beings can protect themselves against the demands of natural selection:

We build asylums for the imbecile, the maimed, and the sick; we institute poor-laws; and our medical men exert their utmost skill to save the life of everyone to the last moment ... Thus the weak members of civilised societies propagate their kind. No one who has attended to the breeding of domestic animals will doubt that this must be highly injurious to the race of man.[5]

Once there is an idea that some human beings are more 'worthy' or 'able' than others, it is only a short step to the thought that it might be best for society if the worthy had more children than the unworthy, and only another short step to the thought that it would be even better if the unworthy had none at all. This idea was at the root of the various eugenics movements which flourished in the early part of the twentieth century. Francis Galton, a founder of eugenics, argued that a successful eugenics policy would result in the human species, as a whole, being

> less foolish, less frivolous, and politically more provident than now. Its demagogues who *'played* to the gallery' would play to a more sensible gallery than at present. We should be better fitted to fulfil our vast imperial opportunities. Lastly, men of an order of ability which is now very rare would become more frequent, because, the level out of which they rose would have itself risen.[6]

To this end, Galton argued that eugenics should be introduced into the national conscience as if it were a new religion.

> The improvement of our stock seems to me one of the highest objects that we can reasonably attempt. We are ignorant of the ultimate destinies of humanity, but feel perfectly sure that it is as noble a work to raise its level ... as it would be disgraceful to abase it. I see no impossibility in eugenics becoming a religious dogma among mankind ...[7]

From a twenty-first century standpoint this sounds almost deranged. But nearly a century ago eugenics was becoming fashionable. Amongst its advocates were H.G. Wells, George Bernard Shaw, Winston Churchill, Beatrice and Sidney Webb, Harold Laski and Virginia Woolf. Bernard Shaw, for example, was moved to declare that 'nothing but a eugenic religion can save our civilization from the fate that has overtaken all previous civilizations'.

It is important to emphasize that eugenics was considered to be an enlightened practice. It was thought not only that it would improve the stock of human beings but also that it would prevent needless suffering; if the lives of the most feeble of human beings are to be *nasty, short* and *brutish*, then it seems to be doing everyone a favour – even the potential most-feeble themselves – to prevent their being born in the first place. However, even in the early stages of the eugenics movement some people worried about where it all might end. For example, at a meeting of the London Sociological Society in 1904, the sociologist Benjamin Kidd, responding to a paper given by Francis Galton, commented on the dangers of a tendency he thought eugenics could foster:

> It might renew, in the name of science, tyrannies that it took long ages of social evolution to emerge from. Judging from what one sometimes reads, many of our ardent reformers would often be willing to put us into lethal chambers, if our minds and bodies did not conform to certain standards.[8]

This kind of concern was sufficiently pronounced that Caleb Saleeby, founder of the English Eugenics Society, felt a need to deny in a lecture in 1909 that eugenics was a philosophy of death:

> Eugenics has nothing to do with killing babies or anyone else. Nature must work by a selective death-rate: Eugenics, the instrument of the moral intelligence of man, replaces it by a selective birth-rate. Eugenics says of every living creature that it has an indefeasible right to live ... killing anybody has nothing to do with Eugenics.[9]

We now know, of course, that the fears which motivated this response were well founded and that Kidd's mention of 'lethal chambers' was all too prescient. Eugenics, taken to its extreme, and combined with a philosophy of racial purity, culminated in the death-camps of Nazi Germany. There is little doubt that Galton and the early eugenicists would have been appalled by this outcome. But it is also clear that their own philosophy was suffused with the same kind of racial thinking which led to the horrors of National Socialism. Galton, for example, in a now famous letter to *The Times* (5 June 1873), declared that 'average negroes possess too little intellect, self-reliance, and self-control to make it possible for them to sustain the burden of any respectable form of civilisation without a large measure of external guidance and support'.

Similarly, in the USA, eugenicists were committed, almost universally, to a philosophy of white racial superiority. In 1916 Madison Grant, a wealthy lawyer, argued in his popular work, *The Passing of the Great Race*, that immigration in the USA was harming American civilization. The new immigrants, he claimed, were physically, intellectually and morally inferior to the peoples of the great 'Nordic' race – the English, Scandinavians, Germans and Irish – who had come to the USA during an earlier wave of immigration.[10] It was worries about racial purity which in part led to the 1924 Immigration Act. The main intention of this Act was to restrict immigration from eastern and southern Europe. Emanuel Celler, a Member of Congress, and opponent of the Act, said of it:

> We were afraid of foreigners; we distrusted them; we didn't like them. Under this act only some one hundred and fifty odd thousands would be permitted to enter the United States. If you were of Anglo-Saxon origin, you could have over two-thirds of the quota numbers allotted to your people. If you were Japanese, you could not come in at all. That, of course, had been true of the Chinese since 1880. If you were southern or eastern European, you could dribble in and remain on sufferance.[11]

Legislation motivated by concerns about racial purity did not end with immigration laws. The US eugenics movement strongly supported laws which outlawed interracial marriage. These had been in existence since the seventeenth century, but the eugenicists pushed for their strengthening and for the introduction of new laws. The 1924 Virginia Racial Integrity Act, for example, was implemented after a campaign by leading eugenicists. It became known as the 'One Drop' Law for the new level of scientific-sounding precision it articulated, as in this provision:

> It shall hereafter be unlawful for any white person in this State to marry any save a white person, or a person with no other admixture of blood than white and American Indian. For the purpose of this act, the term 'white person' shall apply only to the person who has no trace whatsoever of any blood other than Caucasian; but persons who have one-sixteenth

or less of the blood of the American Indian and have no other non-Caucasic blood shall be deemed to be white persons.[12]

One of the most interesting things about eugenical thinking in the USA at this time is that it took on a quasi-scientific form. Charles Davenport, director of the Eugenics Record Office, for example, employed Mendelian principles in order to examine patterns of heritability. In fact, some of his work, even in modern terms, was perfectly respectable; for example, he published sensible papers on the heritability of eye and hair colour.

However, trouble arose when people began to look at the heritability of behavioural and personality traits. Inevitably, then, a whole lot of cultural baggage ended up in the mix. Particularly, it was supposed that traits were distributed, via a germ plasm, along racial lines. Caucasians, as we have seen, were thought to possess the greatest number of admirable traits (intelligence, thriftiness, self-sacrifice, and so on); the other races, in varying proportions, the greatest number of undesirable traits. Hence, a racial prejudice that already existed was able to gain a veneer of scientific respectability, which in turn gave a certain impetus to the political and social agenda of the eugenics movement.

It was not only in the USA that eugenics had an effect on legislation. Many countries, for example, introduced laws which permitted the forcible sterilization of people who had been designated 'unfit' to be parents. Sweden is a case in point; despite its liberal tradition, more than 60,000 women between 1936 and 1976 were forcibly sterilized.[13] In 1999 the Swedish government apologized, and agreed to pay around $21,000 each to the surviving victims of the policy. In fact, in Europe, with the exception of Britain, nearly every country in which the Catholic Church was not a major force introduced sterilization policies of one form or another.[14]

The USA also opted for compulsory sterilization. In 1907 Indiana became the first state to enact sterilization legislation. The declared intention of its statute was 'to prevent procreation of confirmed criminals, idiots, imbeciles, and rapists'. It allowed for the sterilization of people detained within various state institutions (such as prisons and asylums), where a committee of experts had determined that procreation was inadvisable and that there was no possibility of a person's physical or mental improvement. Other states quickly followed suit, but it was after a Supreme Court ruling in 1927, which sanctioned the compulsory sterilization of the mentally defective (in Justice Oliver Wendell Holmes's notorious words, 'three generations of imbeciles are enough'), that sterilization rates increased dramatically. It is estimated that nearly 65,000 people were subject to involuntary sterilization before the practice was finally abandoned in the USA in the 1960s.

It is striking, indeed shocking, that involuntary sterilization continued for such a long time, but the longevity of this particular translation of eugenic thought into practice was the exception rather than the rule. Eugenics was a popular and influential idea but only for a short time: the revelation of what the Nazis did in the name of racial improvement and purity killed that popularity and influence pretty thoroughly after 1945. But there was strong opposition to eugenical ideas even at the height of their popularity: opposition which was linked as both cause and effect to scepticism about the relevance of Darwinian thinking for understanding human nature.

The most influential figure in the rise of scepticism about the relevance of concepts such as human nature and racial superiority was probably the anthropologist Franz Boas. Boas was an interesting and admirable man: a lifelong radical (his mother and aunt were involved in the 1848 revolution in Germany), in his own words an 'unregenerate idealist', who emigrated to the USA and spent much of his life trying to counter fashionable racist thinking there. He argued that the determinations of human behaviour are too complex to be easily separated into biological and social components; and that while heredity might partly explain the differences between *individual* human beings, there was no convincing evidence that it accounts for the variability of cultures. He also rejected the idea that there are significant differences between the abilities of the races:

> If we ask the question whether there is any valid scientific proof for the contention that different races have any kind of genetically determined constitutional disabilities or abilities, we can safely say that we have no evidence supporting this view. Every race has its mentally strong and weak individuals, its great intellects and its idiots, its men and women of strong and weak will power. The existence of any pure race with special endowments is a myth, as is the belief that there are races all of whose members are foredoomed to eternal inferiority.[15]

Boas's arguments influenced some of the most important thinkers of the early and middle parts of the twentieth century. Ruth Benedict, for example, best known for her book *Patterns of Culture*, in which she argued that the behaviour of individuals is overwhelmingly determined by society, was Boas's student at Columbia University. And Margaret Mead, whose *Coming of Age in Samoa* was perhaps the most famous statement of the importance of culture in shaping social behaviour, was a graduate student of both Boas and Benedict.

In his book *In Search of Human Nature*, Carl Degler shows just how profound a shift occurred in American social thought in the middle part of the twentieth century; partly as a result of the influence of scholars such as Boas, Benedict and Mead, behaviour increasingly came to be seen as being decoupled from nature. By the end of the 1950s, biological theories of human behaviour had pretty much disappeared from mainstream view. Degler cites the example of a late-1950s survey, conducted by George Stocking, which looked at social psychological studies dealing with ethnic minorities. Stocking was unable to find a single writer who suggested 'that the personality characteristics of Negroes might be in any part the result of innate racial tendencies'.[16] Degler also notes that the cultural concept was just as dominant in the field of sociology. He quotes, as an example, sociologist Robert Faris on the plasticity of human ability:

> We no longer heed the doctrinaire testers who pronounce specific
> individual limits for potentialities in mechanical ability, language ability,
> artistic ability, and mathematical ability. Their ceilings have been
> discovered to be penetrable ... Barriers in many fields of knowledge are
> falling before the new optimism which is that anybody can learn anything
> ... We have turned away from the concept of human ability as something
> fixed in the physiological structure, to that of a flexible and versatile
> mechanism subject to great improvement.[17]

This turning away from biology is another example of extra-rational
concerns driving interpretation; the evidence base to justify such a
thoroughgoing abandonment of the biological hypothesis simply
did not exist.[18] This was a further instance in the history of
evolutionary thought of theory following ideology. The ideological
commitment was to a philosophy of equality, and it was thought that
it required the rejection of the applicability of Darwinian thinking to
human beings.

It is easy to see how this thought originated. As we have seen,
ideas about biology had been used to buttress social and political
ideals which were predicated upon a valorization of inequality.
Consequently, anyone who was committed to egalitarianism in the
middle part of the twentieth century had good reason to be
suspicious of evolutionary thought. This point, and also the extent to
which a general anti-Darwinism can be motivated by a commitment
to a progressive politics, comes through in an interesting side story
about the famous Scopes trial of 1925.

The trial took place in Dayton, Tennessee, after teacher John
Scopes, acting in alliance with the American Civil Liberties Union, had
deliberately provoked prosecution by teaching Darwinism in
violation of state law. Part of what made the case notable was that
it featured a confrontation between William Jennings Bryan, a former
presidential candidate and fundamentalist Christian, and defence
lawyer Clarence Darrow, who put Bryan on the stand as an expert
witness on the Bible. The usual view of the trial, partly influenced by
the film *Inherit the Wind*, is that Darrow made a fool of Bryan, and

that Christian fundamentalism and biblical inerrancy were significantly undermined as a result. But the truth is probably slightly more complex than this suggests; while Bryan was pilloried in the press, his side actually won the case, and the Tennessee law was not revoked until the 1960s.

The interesting issue for our purposes, though, is the question of Bryan's motivations. He had always been a populist with a radical, progressive streak, supporting, for example, women's suffrage, a progressive taxation system, and pacifism in foreign affairs. And though he had never accepted the truth of Darwin's theory, for most of his life he was not a particular enemy of it. So how did he end up siding with the forces of conservatism on the issue of the teaching of evolution?

Stephen Jay Gould deals with this question in his essay 'William Jennings Bryan's Last Campaign'. He identifies three strands to Bryan's fight against Darwinism.

1. Bryan was worried about the relationship between Darwinist theorizing and the rise of militarism.[19]
2. He thought that Darwinism had persuaded many people of the virtues of selfishness and personal gain; and that to the extent that it contributed to a kind of moral decay, it was likely to result in the greater exploitation of the weak and vulnerable.
3. Bryan argued that since Darwinism was rejected by the majority of people, they had the right to see it excluded from their classrooms.

Gould rejects the third of these strands – truth is not determined by majority opinion – but he argues that there is something in the first two:

> … Bryan was right in one crucial way. Lord only knows, he understood precious little about science, and wins no medals for logic of argument. But when he said that Darwinism had been widely portrayed as a defence of war, domination, and domestic exploitation, he was right. Scientists would not be to blame for this if we had always maintained proper

caution in interpretation and proper humility in resisting the extension of our findings into inappropriate domains. But many of these insidious and harmful misinterpretations had been promoted by scientists.[20]

Gould illustrates this point in a striking way. He quotes from the textbook which John Scopes had used to teach evolution to show that eugenical ideas had made their way into its pages. George William Hunter, the book's author, had this to say about how bad heredity runs in families.

> Hundreds of families such as those described above exist today, spreading disease, immorality and crime to all parts of this country … If such people were lower animals, we would probably kill them off to prevent them from spreading. Humanity will not allow this, but we do have the remedy of separating the sexes in asylums or other places and in various ways preventing intermarriage and the possibilities of perpetuating such a low and degenerate race.[21]

Gould's conclusion about Bryan is that he had correctly identified a problem, but that he had come up with the wrong solution.

The Bryan story shows then that there was little mystery about the turn away from biology which occurred in the early to middle part of the twentieth century. For people committed to a progressive politics, the uses made of Darwinism were unacceptable; it was natural, therefore, that they should look upon evolutionary thinking in general with deep suspicion. If one then adds the impact of the horrors of National Socialism, it is not surprising that in 1959 George Stocking could not find a single social psychologist willing to suggest that the personalities of black people might be genetically determined.

But this situation was never going to last; to the extent that the turn away from biology was motivated by moral and political concerns, it was always likely to be undermined by the facticity of the world. Indeed, within several of the subdisciplines of the humanities and social sciences, interest in biology never entirely disappeared. For example, in the mid 1940s there were a number of conferences for experimental psychologists in the USA which explored the importance of genetics and heredity for the understanding of human behaviour; and, at this time, even among anthropologists, the pioneers of the sociocultural approach, it was possible to find one or two who were willing to reference innate factors in their work.

However, it was really in the 1960s and early 1970s that people began to look again at biological concepts, to see whether they could be successfully incorporated within the various branches of social thought. In the UK, for example, the psychologist Hans Eysenck published books and articles throughout this period which explored the biological basis of personality; and in 1967 zoologist Desmond Morris's book *Naked Ape: A Zoologist's Study of the Human Animal* was a bestseller. Similarly, in the USA at this time, researchers such as Lionel Tiger, Robin Fox, Robert Ardrey, Gardner Lindzey, Roger Masters and George P. Murdock were looking at the uses of biology in disciplines ranging from social psychology to political science.

In terms of the concerns of this chapter, the most interesting thing about this move back towards biology is the reaction it provoked. This is perhaps best illustrated by what happened after the publication in 1975 of Edward O. Wilson's groundbreaking book, *Sociobiology: The New Synthesis*. The major part of this work, reflecting Wilson's expertise in areas such as population biology and ecology, was devoted to explicating the neo-Darwinian under-pinning of animal social behaviour. However, in its last chapter, Wilson turned his attention to *Homo sapiens*, and suggested that human social behaviour was analysable in similar terms.

This suggestion provoked a furious reaction: in Wilson's words, 'the most tumultuous controversy of the 1970s'. A group of Boston scientists, researchers and students – including Richard Lewontin and Stephen Jay Gould, both colleagues of Wilson at Harvard's Museum of Comparative Zoology – formed the Sociobiology Study Group, noting in the *New York Review of Books* that theories which attempted to establish a biological foundation to social behaviour were 'an important basis … for eugenic policies which led to the establishment of gas chambers in Nazi Germany'; the American

Anthropological Association, in a move which *Time* magazine likened to the Catholic Church's denunciation of Galileo, debated a motion to censure sociobiology on the grounds that it was 'an attempt to justify genetically the sexist, racist and elitist status quo in human society'; and protestors from the International Committee against Racism dumped a pitcher of ice water over Wilson himself at a meeting of the American Association for the Advancement of Science in early 1978.

Wilson's opponents were motivated by explicitly moral and political commitments. The Sociobiology Study Group was affiliated to an organization called Science for the People, which was founded in the 1960s to challenge the kinds of science it considered politically dangerous. Lewontin and Gould, both of whom supported the organization's wider aims, considered themselves to be working in the tradition of Marxist theory. Lewontin, in his book *Biology as Ideology*, declared that biological approaches which placed the individual at the centre of their conceptual schemas were 'simply a reflection of the ideologies of the bourgeois revolutions of the eighteenth century that placed the individual at the centre of everything'; and writing with Steven Rose and Leon Kamin in *Not in Our Genes*, he explained their motivations this way:

> We share a commitment to the prospect of the creation of a more socially just – a socialist – society. And we recognise that a critical science is an integral part of the struggle to create that society, just as we also believe that the social function of much of today's science is to hinder the creation of that society by acting to preserve the interests of the dominant class, gender, and race. This belief – in the possibility of a critical and liberatory science – is why we have each in our separate ways and to varying degrees been involved in the development of what has become known over the 1970s and 1980s, in the United States and Britain, as the radical science movement.

It might be tempting to suppose that ideologically motivated criticism of the kinds of ideas espoused in Wilson's *Sociobiology* would come almost inevitably from people who share Lewontin's political outlook; that it would be coterminous with a certain kind of radical, left-wing politics. However, this is not the case, as is illustrated by considering how a debate about Richard Dawkins' book *The Selfish Gene* played out in the journal *Philosophy* at the beginning of the 1980s.

The Selfish Gene is the kind of book which changes the way that people look at the world. Its importance is that it articulates a gene's-eye view of evolution. According to this view, all organisms, including human beings, are 'survival machines' which have been 'blindly programmed' to preserve their genes.[22] Of course, extant survival machines take a myriad of different forms – it is estimated, for example, that there are some three million different species of insect alone – but they all have in common the fact that they have been built according to the instructions of successful genes; that is, genes whose replicas in previous generations managed to get themselves copied.

At the level of genes, things are competitive. Genes that contribute to making good bodies – bodies that stay alive and reproduce – come to dominate a gene pool (the whole set of genes in a breeding population). So, for example, if a gene emerges which has the effect of improving the camouflage of stick-insects, it will in time very probably achieve a preponderance over alternative genes – alleles – which produce less effective camouflage. There are no such things as long-lived, altruistic genes. If a gene has the effect of increasing the welfare of its alleles to its own detriment, it will in the end perish. In this sense, then, all long-lived genes are 'selfish', concerned only with their own survival; and the world is necessarily full of genes which have successfully looked after their own interests.

There are good reasons for seeing evolution as operating at the level of genes. Alternative theories are either unworkable (i.e., group selectionism) or unnecessarily complex (i.e., individual selectionism). However, despite the fact that the central message of *The Selfish Gene* has become scientific orthodoxy, the book, and the ideas associated with it, have gained something of a reputation for extremism. In part, this is because they have been subject to sustained criticism by a number of high-profile, often media-friendly people working in the sciences and humanities. On the science side of things, Steven Rose, Richard Lewontin and Stephen Jay Gould have all attacked Dawkins' ideas. On the humanities side, critics have included, amongst others, David Stove, Hilary Rose and, perhaps most notoriously, Mary Midgley.

Midgley first turned her attention to Dawkins' ideas in an article called 'Gene Juggling' which appeared in *Philosophy* in 1979. On the first page of the article, she had this to say about Dawkins and *The Selfish Gene*:

> His central point is that the emotional nature of man is exclusively self-interested, and he argues this by claiming that all emotional nature is so. Since the emotional nature of animals clearly is not exclusively self-interested, nor based on any long-term calculation at all, he resorts to arguing from speculations about the emotional nature of genes, which he treats as the source and archetype of all emotional nature.[23]

Unfortunately, as Andrew Brown points out in his book *The Darwin Wars*, this is just about as wrong as it is possible to get about selfish gene theory. It is wrong on a number of counts.

(1) Dawkins makes it absolutely clear in *The Selfish Gene* that he is not using the word 'selfishness' – or its opposite 'altruism' – to refer to the psychological states, emotional or otherwise, of any entity. Rather, as he points out in 'In Defence of Selfish Genes', his reply to Midgley, he gives the word an explicitly behaviouristic definition:

> An entity ... is said to be altruistic if it behaves in such a way as to increase another such entity's welfare at the expense of its own. Selfish behaviour has exactly the opposite effect. 'Welfare' is defined as 'chances of survival' ... It is important to realise that the ... definitions of altruism and selfishness are *behavioural*, not subjective. I am not concerned here with the psychology of motives.[24]

There are no grounds, then, for supposing, as Midgley did, that the central message of *The Selfish Gene* has anything to do with the emotional natures of humans, animals or genes.

(2) The very idea that Dawkins might think that genes have an emotional nature is so bizarre that it is hard to know what to make of it. One would be tempted to conclude that Midgley didn't really mean it, except that she started her article in a similar, though slightly more nuanced, fashion: 'Genes cannot be selfish or unselfish, any more than atoms can be jealous, elephants abstract or biscuits teleological. This should not need mentioning, but ... *The Selfish Gene* has succeeded in confusing a number of people about it ...'[25] Whatever she meant, two things are clear: (a) no reputable biologist thinks that genes have an emotional nature; and (b) genes *can* be selfish in the sense that Dawkins – and other sociobiologists – use the term.

(3) Midgley was confused about levels of analysis. It isn't possible to make straightforward claims about the behaviour of organisms from the fact that their genes are selfish. There is no requirement for individual organisms to be selfish in the service of their genes. Indeed, one of the central points of *The Selfish Gene* is precisely that it is possible to explain the *altruistic* behaviour of individual animals in terms of selfish gene theory.

Mistakes of this sort are typical of Midgley's article as a whole. Dawkins, in his response, claimed that the article had 'no good point to make', and argued that the details of her criticisms were incorrect because they were based on a misunderstanding and misapplication of a technical language. This conclusion is echoed by Andrew Brown, who states: 'It has to be said that by the end of Dawkins's piece ... any impartial reader will see that she misunderstood him.'[26] Indeed, Midgley herself has conceded that she should have expressed her objections to *The Selfish Gene* 'more clearly and temperately'.[27]

It is possible to tell a more complicated story than the one we've been outlining in this chapter to explain how it is that Dawkins' ideas

– and indeed those of other sociobiologists – have provoked the kinds of extreme reaction and misunderstanding characterized by Midgley's 'Gene Juggling'. At its most convoluted, this tale would include episodes dealing with scientism, biological determinism, reductionism, metaphor, motives, moral theory, modes of explanation, levels of selection, and more. But lurking at the back of even this story are concerns which are rooted in ideological, moral and political commitments.

Midgley, for example, is explicit that she was worried about the spectre of social Darwinism:

> The unwillingness of many educated people to accept evolutionary concepts fully and apply them to *Homo sapiens* does not just flow from lack of information, which could be remedied by a good clear textbook. It flows from that early, widespread and deep-rooted bunch of misunderstandings of Darwin's ideas, which is called (somewhat misleadingly) Social Darwinism. This consists in supposing that evolution endorses the simple social ethic of devil-take-the-hindmost … [S]ociobiological thinking, especially in its Dawkinsian form, actually reinforces Social Darwinism, both by its language and by some of its substance. This, and not some mysterious personal spite, was what made me indignant.

There is, of course, a sense in which she is right about this: as we have seen, people are worried about the political and moral implications of evolutionary thinking. However, it is important to note that nowadays critics tend not to talk specifically about social Darwinism in relation to sociobiology. Rather, its impact is felt through critics' concern with a constellation of ideas which are linked by the fact that they are presupposed by social Darwinism. Of these, perhaps the most significant are the notion that the behaviour of human beings is solely determined by their biology (what is now called biological or genetic determinism) and the idea that it is possible to invoke biology in order to *justify* particular social or political arrangements.

So is Midgley right in her claim that Dawkins' ideas in *The Selfish*

Gene amount to a kind of social Darwinism? The answer to this question is a simple no. There is nothing in Dawkins' work which remotely adds up to social Darwinism. There are three main reasons why this conclusion is easy to draw.

(1) Dawkins says clearly that he is not, unlike the social Darwinists, advocating any particular way of living. He puts it this way in *The Selfish Gene*:

> I am not advocating a morality based on evolution. I am saying how things have evolved. I am not saying how we humans morally ought to behave ... My own feeling is that a human society based simply on the gene's law of universal ruthless selfishness would be a very nasty society in which to live.[28]

And he has made this same point much more strongly in recent years (perhaps out of fatigue at the persistent misunderstanding of his views). For example, in the title essay first published in his 2003 book *A Devil's Chaplain*, he begins by quoting Darwin: 'Darwin was less than half joking when he coined the phrase Devil's Chaplain in a letter to his friend Hooker in 1856. "What a book a Devil's Chaplain might write on the clumsy, wasteful, blundering low and horridly cruel works of nature."'[29] He then cites George C. Williams and T.H. Huxley saying very similar things, and for contrast, H.G. Wells's 'blood-chilling lines' revelling in what Darwin, Huxley and Williams recoiled from. Then he chooses his side:

> I hear the bleak sermon of the Devil's Chaplain as a call to arms. As an academic scientist I am a passionate Darwinian, believing that natural selection is, if not the only driving force in evolution, certainly the only known force capable of producing the illusion of purpose which so strikes all who contemplate nature. But at the same time as I support Darwinism as a scientist, I am a passionate anti-Darwinian when it comes to politics and how we should conduct our human affairs.[30]

In essence, what Dawkins is doing here is flagging up the 'is/ought gap'; that is, the fact that it is not possible to derive moral statements about how things ought to be from statements about how things are in the world. For example, if it turns out that we are genetically disposed towards murder, it does not follow that we should, therefore, feel free to murder people. Biological facts do not entail moral facts – a point, incidentally, which is ruinous for social Darwinism.

(2) Dawkins explicitly disavows irrevocable 'genetic determinism'; indeed, he has called it 'pernicious rubbish on an almost astrological scale.'[31] Genes affect behaviour. If you want to do Darwinian theorizing, then you've got to look at the effects of genes. But there are no grounds for thinking that these effects are any more intractable than the effects of the environment. Inevitability is not part of the equation. This is how Dawkins puts it in *The Extended Phenotype*:

> Genetic causes and environmental causes are in principle no different from each other. Some influences of both types may be hard to reverse; others may be easy to reverse. Some may be usually hard to reverse but easy if the right agent is applied. The important point is that there is no general reason for expecting genetic influences to be any more irrevocable than environmental ones.[32]

(3) Dawkins' work is rarely specifically about human beings. Rather, he is dealing with general questions to do with evolutionary theory, many of which are only marginally relevant for understanding human behaviour. Moreover, he is on record as saying that he has little interest in human ethics and does not know a great deal about human psychology.[33] Of course, the argument here is *not* that Dawkins' work never has implications for understanding human behaviour. Rather, it is that where it does, it is not usually because human beings are specifically his subject but because humans are evolved animals and *evolution* is his subject.

The ideas of Richard Dawkins, then, cannot be construed as a kind of social Darwinism. However, because social Darwinism, and also the horrors of scientific racism and eugenics, remain fresh in the minds of many people, particularly, but not exclusively, those who occupy the broad spectrum of the political Left, it remains one of the measures used to judge the merits of *any* biological theory thought to have implications for the understanding of human behaviour.[34] Thus, Dawkins' ideas are condemned not because they are social Darwinist, but because social Darwinism, and related ideas, are evils to be sought out and vigorously contested wherever they *might* be found, even if on close examination it turns out that they are not in fact present.

Thus, there exists a mindset amongst certain sectors of the educated public which undermines the proper examination of sociobiological arguments. It is a mindset which subjugates science to political and moral commitments. It results in sociobiological texts being read from a default position of suspicion. Any perception that the arguments they contain might conceivably be co-opted for the purposes of articulating a social Darwinist agenda – however this is construed – is taken as confirmation that this is where the sympathies of the author lie. And the *scientific* merit of sociobiological arguments is assessed in terms of the extent to which they fit with a political and moral agenda governed by notions of equality and common humanity.

It is easy to point to instances where this mindset prevails. For example, it is involved:

- In Mary Midgley's confusion about selfish genes and selfish individuals; in her accusation that Dawkins' 'crude, cheap, blurred genetics ... is the kingpin of his crude, cheap, blurred psychology';[35] and in her statement that her main aim is 'to show people that they can use Darwin's methods on human behaviour without being committed to a shoddy psychology and a bogus political morality'.[36]
- In the furious reaction, detailed above, which greeted the publication of Wilson's *Sociobiology*.
- In Steven Rose, Leon Kamin and Richard Lewontin's claim that 'Science is the ultimate legitimator of bourgeois ideology';[37] and

their argument that 'universities serve as creators, propagators and legitimators of the ideology of biological determinism. If biological determinism is a weapon in the struggle between classes, then the universities are weapons factories, and their teaching and research faculties are the engineers, designers, and the production workers.'[38]

- In Hilary Rose's claims, in *Red Pepper*, that fundamental Darwinists, 'with their talk of biological universals on matters of social difference are a political and cultural menace to feminists and others who care for justice and freedom'; that they are 'obsessed by the desire to reduce organisms (including humans) to one determining entity – the gene'; and that sociobiology 'has a history which varies from the dodgy to the disgusting on sexual difference.'[39]

The ideas of sociobiologists, then, provoke extreme reactions and misunderstanding because their critics believe them to be in conflict with the moral and political commitments the critics hold. This fact stands independently of any considerations about the merit of the kinds of work which people like Edward O. Wilson and Richard Dawkins are doing. As a result, the *public space* for the debate about evolutionary ideas is polluted by the hyperbole which almost inevitably occurs when the politically engaged feel their baseline commitments to be under threat.

There is something slightly paradoxical and ironic about all this; in terms of their personal politics, both Wilson and Dawkins are a long way from being apologists for untrammelled capitalism. Edward O. Wilson, for example, has had this to say about George Bush's first administration:

Minimal government is part of the philosophy of the current brand of right-wing conservatism. Their claim is that there is too much government in the United States. They argue that it is necessary to cut down on bureaucracy and regulation, in order to return power to the people. I won't comment on this disastrous way of thinking![40]

Similarly, Richard Dawkins implored Americans not to re-elect George Bush in 2004:

> As the bumper stickers put it, 'Re-defeat Bush.' But, this time, do it so overwhelmingly that neither his brother's friends in Florida nor his father's friends on the Supreme Court will be able to rig the count. Decent Americans ... please show your electoral muscle this time around.[41]

And in the second edition of *The Selfish Gene*, Dawkins noted that he had helped to vote in a socialist government in 1974; and said of Thatcherism that it 'elevated meanness and selfishness to the status of ideology'.[42]

In effect, then, when the critics of sociobiology allege that Wilson and Dawkins provide support for the more egregious aspects of capitalism, the claim must be that their work reflects, disseminates and perpetuates a set of social and political ideas for which neither scientist has any great personal sympathy. It must be said that there is nothing contradictory in this claim. The argument that people unwittingly reflect bourgeois ideology, for example, has long been a standard part of the Marxist armoury. But there is something deeply ironic about it. As we have seen in this chapter, the history of evolutionary thought is dominated by ideas which meld the biological with the social in ways which fit the political and ideological commitments of their advocates. Thus, social Darwinists justified their commitment to *laissez-faire* capitalism in terms of ideas to do with the survival of the fittest; scientific racists used biology to bolster their racial prejudice; Boas, and his followers, rejected biological explanations of human behaviour because of perceived threats to a politics of egalitarianism; and, as we have seen, the opponents of sociobiology frame their objections in terms of a commitment to 'critical and liberatory science' and the possibility of expunging a 'crude political morality' from Darwinian theorizing.

The irony is that in this company it is the sociobiologists who carry the least political baggage around with them. The critics of Wilson and Dawkins might see them as the biological division of the ideological state apparatus of bourgeois capitalism, but the reality is that politics just isn't their main concern; certainly, in contrast to many of their opponents, they do not allow their own political commitments to drive their scientific work. Indeed, Dawkins has suggested that *The Selfish Gene* isn't really about human beings at all:

> I think that some people just cannot conceive of anybody not being fundamentally interested in humans, so they assume that everything that you say must have human significance, and must have been intended to have human significance. They just cannot grasp that there are some interesting questions to be asked about evolutionary theory itself which may have very little connection with humans. Now that is disputable, some people think that it is very important for humans and some people don't, but I wasn't committing myself on that. I wasn't even very interested in it.[43]

This is not to argue that sociobiologists never consider the political and sociological implications of their work; Wilson, for example, has certainly argued that biological facts have implications for the way that human beings organize their lives. Nor is it to argue that modern sociobiological arguments are not sometimes employed for dubious political ends: clearly this happens. It is rather to insist that sociobiologists are no more guilty than their critics in these regards; and frequently they are a good deal less guilty.

There is a final point to make here which has to do with wishful thinking. There is something troubling about people's almost childish desire to reconstruct the world imaginatively so that it fits neatly with their wider beliefs and values. This phenomenon is entirely familiar when it comes, for example, to the practice of maintaining religious belief in the face of countervailing scientific evidence; just consider, for instance, the absurdities of Philip Gosse's and Duane Gish's separate attempts to show that the fossil record supports biblical literalism; or the increasingly desperate efforts on the part of people such as Michael Behe to show that living organisms manifest the kind of 'irreducible complexity' which requires an intelligent designer. However, the fact that it is also prevalent in arguments about biology, evolution and human beings is more disheartening. The idea that nature will be amenable to the construction of a 'critical and liberatory science' is a clear case of wishful thinking; as was the idea that the supposed moral superiority of white races is grounded in biology; as is the notion that human beings in a state of nature are 'noble savages', corrupted only through their exposure to Western civilization; and as is the idea that human nature is thoroughly malleable, thereby guaranteeing equality if the environment is right.

Wishful thinking of various stripes has coloured the debate about evolution and human nature from the very beginning. This is not likely to change in the near future. In the meantime, then, the best advice for sober scholars, for people who think that matters of fact should be decided on the basis of the evidence rather than ideology, is that they should treat those theories which set up a neat correspondence between the wished-for and the real with extreme suspicion.

6 Wishful Thinking and Epistemological Confusion

In the July 1986 edition of the now defunct *Marxism Today*, Stuart Hall and Martin Jacques argued that a new kind of politics was sweeping the UK.[1] It was, they claimed, rooted in the various charity events which had taken place over the previous twelve months: Band Aid, Live Aid and Sport Aid. This new kind of politics, we were told, offered an alternative vision of society, organized around a dynamic of 'caring', and it represented a severe blow to the ideology of selfishness which underpinned Thatcherism. Hall and Jacques' optimism was shortlived, however; by December 1986, they were arguing that even those people opposed to Thatcherism were not 'for' anything else in particular; and that there was no end in sight to the 'nightmare' of Conservative government.[2]

Fast-forward some seventeen years, and it is possible to find Madeleine Bunting arguing in the *Guardian* that the demonstration against the Iraq War which occurred in London on 15 February 2003 represented a defining moment in contemporary political culture. After such a day, she informed us, it was so much harder to speak of the selfish individualism of consumer society. And about the consequences of a war in Iraq, she opined: 'What happens once the orphans, the widowed and the killed appear on our screens? Then, the stubbornness will become anger. We said No, Not in our Names and we meant it. Blair will never be forgiven. A tragic end to a good prime minister ...'[3]

The point about these two stories is that they are indicative of a wishful thinking which all too easily infects political analysis. It might have appeared to Hall and Jacques in the summer of 1986 that the hegemony of Thatcherism had been broken, but a year later the Conservatives under Margaret Thatcher were re-elected to government with a majority of 102. And to some of the people marching through London early in 2003, it might have seemed that they were part of a new kind of political mobilization, but six months later similar events attracted only a tiny fraction of the number who attended the February demonstration.

Wishful thinking of course is not a monopoly of the Left. Libertarians rely on some highly dubious notions of human rationality, of universal access to complete and disinterested information, of the market's ability to solve all problems, and the like. Conservatives irritated by some of the products of modernity like to counter Whiggish, progressive accounts of history with a version in which the present is a dreadful falling-off from the Garden of Eden or Golden Age, when people knew their places and everything was bliss.

In short, any kind of political theorizing is by its very nature likely to include an element of wishful thinking. Wishful thinking is in a sense fundamental to political thinking, is woven into the very heart of it. At least, into any political theorizing and tendency that is at all reformist in its views, as opposed to simply more of the same please. Political thought in other words generally includes a prescriptive element as well as a descriptive. It is about ought as well as is – that is part of what Left and Right *mean*: we should do this, or alternatively that. That is why phrases like leftist biologist or conservative geologist sound (or should sound) peculiar, or oxymoronic, as we noted in Chapter 3. Geology and astronomy are not op-ed subjects; the truth or falsity of their findings cannot be determined by a vote.

Reformist political thinking is about change, and human efforts to make change. In order to conceive of, argue for, and make political change, one has to think about it: one has to imagine that things could be otherwise. One has to entertain counterfactuals, look at alternatives, ponder thought experiments. In a sense one has to tell lies. Hannah Arendt pointed this out in an essay on the Pentagon Papers in 1971, in which she noted that truthfulness has never been thought a political virtue, and that it is surprising how little attention philosophers and political theorists have paid to the significance of this fact for our capacity to second-guess what happens to be the case.

> In order to make room for one's own action, something that was there before must be removed or destroyed, and things as they were before are changed. Such change would be impossible if we could not mentally remove ourselves from where we physically are located and *imagine* that things might as well be different from what they actually are. In other words, the deliberate denial of factual truth – the ability to lie – and the capacity to change facts – the ability to act – are interconnected; they owe their existence to the same source: imagination.[4]

Looked at from this angle, this ability to think the thing which is not is an essential human ability; without it nothing could ever improve except by accident. It is a good thing. But it is also the crack by which wishful thinking gets in. We want things to be better – so we may start to delude ourselves that it won't be too terribly difficult to make them better.

One key way we do this is by insisting on the infinite plasticity of human nature. Any change in social arrangements is at least possible, because there is nothing built into our natures that would rule that 'anything' out. It may be that left-wing thought is more dependent on this view than right-wing thought. Conservatives (though not libertarians and anarchists, who can be either Right or Left) tend to emphasize human limits and limitations, which in the case of religious conservatives translates to Original Sin. Progressives tend to emphasize Romantic notions of human perfectibility and glorious potential.

Progressive thinking of this kind is founded on the Lockean view that human beings are blank slates; that whatever one finds in their minds has come in from the outside. The importance of this doctrine is that it allows the possibility of the perfectibility of humankind. If people behave badly – if they harm each other in various ways, for example – it is because of distorted social relations; or a breakdown in the normative system of society. It is not because they are dispositionally inclined towards aggression or selfishness. It is possible, therefore, to look forward to the day when human beings will live in harmony with each other; if you get society right, then you will get people right.

However, the trouble with this view is that it runs contrary to a wealth of evidence which suggests that *Homo sapiens* is far from being a blank slate.[5] And, of course, one result of holding to a view which flies in the face of the evidence is that you very quickly get into difficulties if you try to build a political theory on top of it. This is perhaps best illustrated by the case of Marxism.

It is debatable whether Karl Marx was committed to a genuinely blank-slate view of human nature. However, he was certainly in the spirit of this view with his argument that the ills of society, and indeed of humankind, are ultimately a function of the way in which production is organized; that is, that they are societal – or material – in origin. Two key concepts drive this argument: *class conflict* and *alienation*. It was Marx's claim that all *hitherto existing* societies have been based on a fundamental conflict between those who own and control the means of production and those who don't. In capitalism, this means a conflict between two great antagonistic classes: the bourgeoisie (the owners of the means of production) and the proletariat (who own only their own labour power). In this scheme, the proletariat are the bearers of the emancipatory potential of humankind. As a collectivity, a *class-for-itself*, they hold the ability – indeed, in some versions of Marxism it is their destiny – to abolish all class distinctions, instituting a new form of society based on collective ownership; in doing so, they will end the alienation of people from the products of their labour, from the labour process itself and from their species-being.

At base, Marxism is just another utopian theory, albeit dressed up in some fancy philosophical clothes. Communism is posited as the end state of history; it is a form of social existence devoid of systematic conflict and antagonism. People in communist society – rational, self-aware and other-regarding – will no longer be estranged from each other or themselves. Thus, Friedrich Engels envisaged a day when state power and the government of people will not be necessary:

> *The proletariat seizes political power and turns the means of production into State property.*
>
> But, in doing this, it abolishes itself as proletariat, abolishes all class distinction and class antagonisms, abolishes also the State as State. Society, thus far, based upon class antagonisms, had need of the State ... As soon as there is no longer any social class to be held in subjection; as soon as class rule, and the individual struggle for existence based upon our present anarchy in production, with the collisions and excesses arising from these, are removed, nothing more remains to be repressed, and a special repressive force, a State, is no longer necessary ... State interference in social relations becomes, in one domain after another, superfluous, and then dies out of itself; the government of persons is replaced by the administration of things, and by the conduct of processes of production. The State is not 'abolished'. *It dies out.*[6]

The major problem with this vision of a future without conflict is that it is predicated on the highly implausible claim that one can eradicate strife from human social relations simply by altering the material conditions in which people live. In other words, it is a *prima-facie* example of wishful thinking. There is, for example, a wealth of evidence which suggests, *contra* Marx, that violence and aggression are an ineluctable part of the human condition. Here's Steven Pinker on this matter:

Violence is a human universal, including murder, rape, grievous bodily harm and theft. It is found in *all* cultures. Also, contrary to the belief of many intellectuals, the best ethnographic accounts show that the highest rates of violence are found in pre-state, foraging societies. Rates of homicide and death by warfare in these societies are, by orders of magnitude, higher than in the modern West.

Even in Western societies, a majority of people harbour violent fantasies about people they don't like, though of course most never act on them. Also, violence appears early in the life of a child – the majority of two year olds kick, bite and scratch ... When you put all this together, it suggests that at least the urge to violence, if not necessarily violence itself, is part of our nature. It's a desire that is present in most people and a behaviour option which we take up easily.[7]

The Marxist misreading of human nature makes its vision of a conflict-free future society implausible. It also undermines the analyses which Marxists offer up of social and political phenomena, a result which puts the reliability of the Marxist analytical framework in doubt. The position of women in society is perhaps the classic example.

The problem for Marxism is that it is far from obvious that sexual inequality is at bottom to do with the mode of production; or that the abolition of private property, and the advent of a communist society, will bring an end to sexual inequality. The standard Marxist line, set out primarily in Engels' *The Origin of the Family, Private Property and the State*, is that the oppression of women is a function of their confinement within the domestic sphere; something which exists in order to ensure clear lines of descent so that men can pass on property to their natural heirs. In Engels' words: 'the sole exclusive aims of monogamous marriage were to make the man supreme in the family, and to propagate, as the future heirs to his wealth, children indisputably his own.'[8] The implication, of course, is that if you abolish private property, then you will remove the material basis for the oppression of women, thereby establishing the grounds for equality between the sexes. So Engels argues that 'The supremacy of the man in marriage is the simple consequence of his economic supremacy, and with the abolition of the latter will disappear of itself'.[9] But, as with the case of social conflict, the difficulty with this view is that it is naïve to think that economics explains all. Particularly, it is just wishful thinking to suppose that innate factors play no part in the story of sexual inequality. Helena Cronin, for example, points out that because natural selection has favoured males with an appetite for multiple mates and a disposition to strive for them, men have a greater tendency than women to be

> competitive, risk-taking, opportunistic, persevering, single-minded, inclined to display, to show off. That is why men are more likely to die heroically, win a Nobel prize, drive too fast, commit murder … It is why such male excess is universal, transcending huge divides of nationality, culture, ethnicity, religion, politics, class and education; and why it manifests itself in modern societies across the globe and in every known record back through time.[10]

It is important to emphasize that to argue that innate factors very probably play a part in sexual inequality is not to make a moral argument for the existence of sexual inequality. Nor is it to argue that sexual inequality is inevitable: Richard Dawkins, for example, has pointed out that there is no reason in principle to suppose that behavioural patterns rooted in genetic differences are any more difficult to alter than behavioural patterns rooted in environmental factors. However, it is to argue that innate factors make a difference, and that it is necessary to take them into account if one wants to develop a political strategy which is likely to be effective in eradicating sexual inequality; and that Marxism, to the extent that it fails to take into account the biological nature of human beings, necessarily produces a flawed understanding of human relationships.

It is, however, perhaps slightly unfair to hold Marx and Engels up to the standards of twenty-first-century knowledge when accusing them of wishful thinking and flawed understanding. Not least, they had not experienced the horrors of the twentieth century when they were putting their theories together. It is not implausible to think that with the kind of hindsight that the last century produced, they might have been less optimistic about human potential and the possibilities for a world without conflict.

Difference feminism and women's ways of knowing

But hope springs eternal, the bromide tells us. And that's reasonable enough, even apart from the psychological need for at least minimal optimism in order to keep functioning. Hope, after all, is to do with the future, and the future is unknown and full of contingencies, which makes room for hope (as well as fear). There's always tomorrow, next year in Jerusalem, and so on.

We noted above that the Left tends to favour the Whig idea of history as progress, amelioration, the things-are-getting-better view, while the Right is often partial to the Golden Age, not so fast, things-are-getting-worse view. Feminism, as a reformist, ameliorative body of thought, thus may have a built-in tendency to valorize suggestions of novelty and renewal. In short, to thinking that the latest version of everything is and must be the best – that 'latest' and 'best' are in some sense the same thing. Second-wave feminism had a tendency to consider its own views on the subjection of women as more radical than those of its predecessors, which is understandable coming at the end of a long period when feminist ideas had largely gone into hiding. But the fact is that some early, or first-wave, feminists were more radical in many ways than much of today's mainstream or popular feminism, which has become less radical in many ways than it was 30-odd years ago.

Perhaps the central question for feminism is: is there anything about women, anything inherent in their natures – in their bodies, their minds, their capabilities, their psychology – that makes unequal laws, status, treatment, customs necessary? Desirable? Fair? Useful? The question of course was for millennia answered in the affirmative.

There were what are now called 'essentialist' reasons – there were true facts about the peculiar, different nature of women – that made their subordination necessary and desirable. They bore children, they were weaker, smaller, stupider, more emotional, more sexual, less rational, and so on. The reply of feminists early and late was that, given that no one had ever done any controlled experiments to see what women's nature might be under conditions of equality, it was not possible to tell what their nature was. Mill put it this way:

> Standing on the ground of common sense and the constitution of the human mind, I deny that anyone knows, or can know, the nature of the two sexes, as long as they have only been seen in their present relation to one another ... What is now called the nature of women is an eminently artificial thing – the result of forced repression in some directions, unnatural stimulation in others ... [A] hot-house and stove cultivation has always been carried on of some of the capabilities of their nature, for the benefit and pleasure of their masters. Then, because certain products of the general vital force sprout luxuriantly and reach a great development in this heated atmosphere and under this active nurture and watering, while other shoots from the same root, which are left outside in the wintry air, with ice purposely heaped all round them, have a stunted growth, and some are burnt off with fire and disappear; men, with that inability to recognise their own work which distinguishes the unanalytic mind, indolently believe that the tree grows of itself in the way they have made it grow, and that it would die if one half of it were not kept in a vapour bath and the other half in the snow.[11]

This argument has something in common with the blank-slate view, but there is also an important difference. The idea is that women's treatment – their systematic subordination and deprivation – has been different enough that it has distorted and suppressed their real natures and capacities in a way that men's natures and capacities have generally not been distorted. In short, that women have been deliberately stunted while men have not, and that therefore there is a genuine epistemological problem about how to know what real limitations women as a group may have.

The idea does leave room for the kind of wishful thinking we discussed above, and heated arguments rage over this territory all the time. Why are there still so few women in physics, mathematics, engineering? Is it because of the statistical tail-end effect? That is, that while average abilities of women and men in those fields are roughly similar, there are more men at the very high (as well as very low) end? Or is it because those fields are still boys' clubs, where men keep hiring other men and they all work unsocial hours? One is an essentialist answer, the other is a social constructivist answer; either or both may be right; debate rages.

There is room here for wishful thinking, and a standing temptation to it, but the idea that women's nature has been distorted by subordination and inequality doesn't *require* wishful thinking or denial. There is a large and significant difference between saying women have no nature, that they are, like all humans, blank slates, and saying that whatever nature they have has been distorted by social and cultural factors.

This view of the matter – call it the Millean view for convenience – sees women as *artificially* subordinate and inferior; as both seen as, and raised to be, dependent, weak and timorous. It considers this a bad state of affairs, and wants to change it: wants to change the expectations and upbringing of women, and women themselves.

But another branch of feminism grew up alongside the Millean variety during the rise of second-wave feminism. It was partly a defensive response to the outraged reactions of many *women* to second-wave feminism, women who claimed that feminists despised and sneered at traditional women who were wives and mothers and nothing further, and happy to be so. There was a good deal of embarrassed backtracking and hand-wringing in the face of this reaction, and 'difference' feminism seemed to be one way to make amends. It also meant there was less work to do (always an incentive for wishful thinking). Difference feminism takes the opposite tack from Millean feminism: it claims that women are indeed different from men – and better; that they are, in many ways, superior, possessing special wisdom, insight and knowledge, often precisely because of their upbringing, even because of their subordination. For example, Sandra Harding, having noted that the 'distinctive features of women's situation in a gender-stratified society are being used as resources in the new feminist research', argues that

> Thinking from the perspective of women's lives makes strange what had appeared familiar, which is the beginning of any scientific enquiry ... Why is this gender difference a scientific resource? It leads us to ask questions about nature and social relations from the perspective of devalued and neglected lives.[12]

Along with its utility for soothing the feelings of non-feminist and traditionalist women, difference feminism is also something of a labour-saving device. If all that is required to improve the status of women is a sort of Nietzschean reversal of values, such that qualities like emotionality and sympathy are declared sources of superior wisdom rather than disabling flaws, then there is considerably less work to do and less resistance to overcome. This fact looks like a strong incentive for wishful thinking.

Given that women are underrepresented in the sciences, mathematics and engineering, that they are almost everywhere the primary care-givers, and that they tend to be excluded from higher managerial and executive positions, one might expect feminists to argue for a change in the material conditions of their existence. One might think they would argue that this kind of inequality should be eradicated by changing the expectations of men and women about women's capabilities, legislating to prevent discrimination on the grounds of sex, and ensuring that there is genuine equality in learning and education.

But difference feminists are ambivalent about one or more of these approaches. There is a worry that 'success' in certain institutions which are seen as especially male – the military, corporations, science – merely co-opts women into institutions which they had nothing to do with establishing or shaping, and simply absorbs women into a male world, leaving it unchanged, rather than altering that world and improving it via the presence of people with fundamentally different ways of seeing the world. Thus difference feminists see the desire for this kind of equality as colluding with male ways of thinking. They are sceptical about the idea that there are some qualities which are desirable for all competent adults; that there are universal goods. Consequently, there is no contradiction in their calling for the valorization of specifically female qualities, while being at best ambivalent about those qualities seen as male – for example, a concern with logic, rationality and abstraction – and about the value of lives predicated upon them.

This approach has the advantage of validating, not to say flattering, the situations and choices of women as they already are, and it also sidesteps the need for radical transformation of existing social arrangements. Women are splendid, here and now, and men should only be so lucky as to be more like women. But the approach has the *disadvantage* that it posits large, far-reaching, hard-wired and essentialist differences between women and men, differences of a scope and significance for which there is little or no real evidence.

Yet despite the shakiness of the idea and its lack of empirical foundation, it has been and is very popular and influential, especially since the 1982 publication of Carol Gilligan's *In a Different Voice*. Gilligan there claims that women have their own version of morality which is rooted in relationships and caring, rather than abstract notions of justice and equity.

It is striking how similar this sounds to the essentialist ideas about women which forbade them entry to public life in the nineteenth century, because they were too good for that profane arena. And indeed, many consider it quite a feat of legerdemain to take what had been thought a classic bit of sexist mystification and turn it into new feminist wisdom. Margaret Talbot commented in the *New Republic*:

[Gilligan's] notion of a feminine morality – more solicitous of feelings than consistent with principles – is, of course, an old one. It is the idea that informed the Victorian conception of separate spheres, of the angel in the house gently shaping an insular dominion that was the very opposite of the striving and impersonal world beyond its walls. Gilligan's teaching is in many ways reactionary, which also helps to account for its extraordinary success.[13]

But however strange this argument may seem, and though her research has been sharply criticized, Gilligan's views are well entrenched in academic Women's Studies departments, especially in the USA. The criticisms were in small academic publications, while Gilligan received admiring attention from mass circulation magazines such as *Time* and the *New York Times Magazine*. In a *Different Voice* inspired such followers as Nell Noddings' *Caring*, Sara Ruddick's *Maternal Thinking* and Belenky, Clinchy, Goldberger and Tarule's *Women's Ways of Knowing*.

The last-named book, based on interviews with 135 women, claims that women are uncomfortable with argument and disagreement, and that they have a different approach to knowledge which emphasizes collaboration, consensus and mutual understanding. *Women's Ways of Knowing* declares in the final paragraph:

We have argued in this book that educators can help women develop their own authentic voices if they emphasise connection over separation, understanding and acceptance over assessment, and collaboration over debate ... if instead of imposing their own expectations and arbitrary requirements, they encourage students to evolve their own patterns of work based on the problems they are pursuing.[14]

Susan Haack points out that the authors '*told their subjects ahead of time* that the interviews in which they were participating were for the purpose of studying their special "women's ways of knowing"; making it impossible to be sure that their responses weren't biased by suggestion'.[15] So the evidence for the claim that women actually have a different 'way of knowing' is not very strong, and studies that came after *Women's Ways of Knowing* have not found much.

And even if there were good evidence for the claim that women think radically differently from the way men do, what would follow from that finding is a separate question. It is not self-evident that the best response is to declare such 'ways of knowing' equal or superior to the array of methods, protocols, reviews, checks, and precautions that have been worked out over the past four centuries in order to minimize the role of human emotion and bias in empirical enquiry. In fact, given that human emotion and bias – however valuable and desirable in other contexts, however important for psychic health and decently other-regarding relationships – are well known to distort enquiry in myriad ways, it seems more reasonable to say that such ways of knowing, if they exist, should be at least supplemented if not trained out of existence by remedial education. In morality, ethics, social life and friendship there may be something to be said for preferring understanding and acceptance to judgement and assessment; but in epistemology or ways of knowing, there is very little.

Noretta Koertge and Daphne Patai make this point in a sly way in *Professing Feminism*:

> *Women's Ways of Knowing* effectively documents the severe learning disabilities some women bring with them to Women's Studies classrooms: Such students may be silent, they may speak only by parroting authorities; some may lapse into a solipsistic state of subjectivity; others may be so fragile that they cannot learn without receiving constant support and approbation. The authors make a strong case for the contention that some women have been epistemologically crippled, but they offer no foundation for any claim that the previously ignored 'ways of knowing' bestow power on women.[16]

The scientific revolution has brought unprecedented increases in human knowledge. The cognitive capacities that propelled that revolution stand in stark contrast to the qualities – nurturing, maternal, empathic – that difference feminists attribute to women. If one wants to test which of two hypotheses most accurately describes the world, then acceptance, love and sympathy are not going to do the job; it requires at least the ability to discriminate, judge and reject.

At the beginning of his book *Science: A History*, John Gribbin notes that the nature of science is such that almost any of his readers could have made the discoveries which constitute scientific progress – in his eyes, perhaps the greatest human achievement – had they been in the right place at the right time. It is startling then to think that there are at least some feminist theorists who are required to claim that this is only the case for Gribbin's male readers. It is certainly the kind of thought which troubles the more traditional kind of feminists. Janet Radcliffe Richards puts it this way:

> It is hard to imagine anything better calculated to delight the soul of patriarchal man than the sight of women's most vociferous leaders taking an approach to feminism that continues so much of his own work: luring women off into a special area of their own where they will remain screened from the detailed study of philosophy and science to which he always said they were unsuited, teaching them indignation instead of argument, fantasy and metaphor instead of science, and doing all this by continuing his very own technique of persuading women that their true interests lie elsewhere than in the areas colonised by men.[17]

The first problem, then, with the argument that women have their own distinctive voices, or their own 'ways of knowing', is that even if it were true, it is not at all clear that it would be a good thing. The second problem is that there is actually no good evidence that it is true; certainly not the kind of evidence which would satisfy Carl Sagan's injunction, echoing Hume, that extraordinary claims require extraordinary evidence.

Consoling fictions

So wishful thinking, in addition to its bad epistemic and cognitive effects, can have perverse political consequences, such as difference feminists consigning women to roles that Millean feminists have long fought to free them from – but perhaps there are other results of wishful thinking that make it not entirely a bad thing. Perhaps a modicum of group wishful thinking can elevate people's self-esteem, thus increasing their confidence, optimism, sense of possibility and capability, and therefore overall happiness and flourishing. It has become conventional wisdom – although there are new studies which cast doubt on the truth of that wisdom – that high self-esteem is necessary for achievement and wellbeing. If this is true, might it not be worth the risk of wishful thinking to promote, for instance, some inaccurate but consoling myths about history in order to encourage pride in a disadvantaged group?

There is already a slight paradox in the idea, because self-esteem would seem to be by definition an individual rather than a group psychic resource. Self-esteem would appear to have to do with the individual self's sources of pride rather than with the group's. But then, anyone who has ever met or been a football fan knows that people do in fact derive a great deal of self-esteem, however vicarious and mediated, from the triumphs and victories of other people, so long as the other people are defined as members of the group the self belongs to.

As with sport – be it the Olympics or Saturday's football game – so with history. Vicarious pride is vicarious pride. So if a group has been kicked around for years, it can be consoling to think 'Yes, but my ancestors were royalty while yours were digging up turnips in the rain'. Thus there is a natural temptation to start telling stories about royal ancestors, even in the absence of any evidence. After all, if there's no evidence – it *might* be true. So why not?

The problem is that history is not the same thing as wishful-history. The word 'history' itself derives from the Greek '*historein*', which means both 'research' and 'enquiry'. History is not simply a narrative about the past; it is a research-driven form of empirical enquiry. Mythic or invented or wishful 'history' is thus not history at all, but a different thing – a branch of literature or story-telling.

History is not propaganda, myth-making or a self-esteem inflation device, though it has often been pressed into service for those tasks. History is highly interpretive, to be sure, but it is always, when done properly, grounded in evidence. The questions are empirical ones, and the interpretation is of evidence, not of daydreams or fantasies.

But there has been quite a lot of glorious-past-invention in the name of history recently. Afrocentrism, Hindutva, Chief Sealth's speech, and Rigoberta Menchu, among others, have all done their bit to inspire and encourage the disadvantaged of the earth. But at a cost. Confusions between myth and history, story and reality, always have a cost, to the ability to think critically if nothing else. As John McWhorter points out in his essay 'We Don't Learn Our History!':

> Blacks of all persuasions labour under remnants of the white perception of blacks as mentally inferior. To embrace – or even let pass – a historical 'framework' with no factual basis only reinforces this. How realistic is it to expect to be accepted as mental equals when blacks presenting themselves as 'professors' chart our history with mythical narratives, as if we were preliterate hunter-gatherers?[18]

And once the confusions are discovered and made public, the cost is even higher. It is difficult to know which is more destructive to group and individual self-esteem in such a case: whether it is the scepticism of those who refuse to go on believing discredited myths, or the 'kind' indulgence of the defenders of myth-making and other people's 'ways of knowing'. It may actually be the latter which is the most corrosive in the long run.

The Afrocentric turn

Afrocentrism is a movement and a school of thought, popular in the USA, which originated with Marcus Garvey in the early twentieth century. Its main focus is opposition to perceived Eurocentrism, which it enacts by emphasizing the achievements of the ancient

Egyptians, whom Afrocentrists view as black. There are elements of anti-Semitism, and the more ideological exponents further claim that Greek philosophy was not Greek at all but was largely borrowed or 'stolen' from the Egyptians.

Afrocentrists have a strong presence in rap and hip-hop culture (and in prisons), as well as in universities and some school districts (local government bodies which administer state schools). School districts are in the mix because, since minority groups are statistically underrepresented in the sciences, educators are always keen to find ways to encourage the interest of such groups in scientific subjects. One hopeful idea was the publication in 1987 of the *African-American Baseline Essays* by the school district in Portland, Oregon. The essays were intended to provide teachers with background information about the knowledge and cultural contributions of Africans and African-Americans, to include as part of their teaching. It sounds a good and benevolent plan, but the essays themselves were not notable for accuracy or sound scholarship.

The anthropologist Bernard Ortiz De Montellano, for example, criticized one of the *Baseline Essays* in detail in two articles for the *Skeptical Inquirer* in 1991 and 1992,[19] and in another article for the New York Academy of Sciences anthology *The Flight from Science and Reason* in 1996.[20] The essay in question, by Hunter Havelin Adams, who was listed as a research scientist but was in fact an industrial hygiene technician with a high school diploma, argues for the scientific validity of the paranormal, and advocates the use of religion as a part of the scientific paradigm. Among other things, the essay claims that there is a distinction between non-scientific magic and scientific 'psychoenergetics', but it does not give a basis for distinguishing one from the other.[21]

Ortiz de Montellano points out that Adams fails to distinguish among sources: scholarly books and journals, popular newspapers and magazines, vanity press books, and 'New Age' publications are all discussed on the same level. Adams says that the nature of science depends on who does it, and that science includes the supernatural.

He refers to parapsychology as science, and claims that ancient Egyptians could predict pregnancy by urinating on barley seeds, that they anticipated many of the philosophical aspects of quantum theory, that they knew the particle/wave nature of light, that the Dogon, an indigenous tribe of Mali, discovered the star Syrius B 500 years ago, and more. Ortiz de Montellano goes on:

> For example, on the basis of a creation myth in which the word *evolved* is used, the *Baseline Essay* claims that Egyptians had a theory of species evolution 'at least 2,000 years before Charles Darwin developed his theory'. On the basis of a 6" × 7" tailless, bird-shaped object found in the Cairo Museum, supposedly a scale model of a glider, Adams says that Egyptians had full-size gliders 4,000 years ago and 'used their early planes for travel, expeditions, and recreation'.[22]

Unfortunately, as Ortiz de Montellano points out, not all school districts have the knowledge to detect the errors in the *Baseline Essays*, and in their eagerness to further the goal of minority participation in science education, some have adopted the essays. Mary Lefkowitz has reported that

> Revisionist Afrocentric curricula have been adopted in schools in Atlanta, Pittsburgh, Washington, D.C., Detroit, Cleveland, Indianapolis, Kansas City, and also at some universities, among them Temple University, Kent State, California State at Long Beach, Cornell University, and Wellesley College.[23]

Lefkowitz is a classics scholar, author of the influential *Women in Greek Myth* and of *The Lives of the Greek Poets*, the research for which required her to study the ways ancient writers 'created historical "facts" to serve particular purposes, some of them political'.[24] She was unfamiliar with Afrocentrism until 1991, when the *New Republic* asked her to write a review-article about Martin Bernal's *Black Athena* and its relation to the Afrocentrist movement – an assignment which, she reports, literally changed her life. She realized the subject was one which required all the attention she could give to it.[25] Once she began doing research for the article she discovered there were books in circulation claiming that Socrates and Cleopatra were of African descent, and that Greek philosophy had actually been stolen from Egypt. The books were popular, and some of the ideas they contained were being taught in schools and universities – including her own Wellesley College. She had thought that Wellesley's longstanding course 'Africans in Antiquity' was about historical Africa, but she discovered it was actually a 'Socrates and Cleopatra were black' course.

Lefkowitz was amazed that her *New Republic* article 'provoked hostility far beyond the range of ordinary scholarly disagreement' and to find herself accused of racist motivation, of leading a 'Jewish onslaught', and of a 'projection of Eurocentric hegemony'.[26] Even more disturbingly, her local academic community did little to help: her questions were not encouraged, and there was no sense that the faculty 'were all involved in a cooperative enterprise'. On the contrary, intellectual debate was 'actively discouraged, even though the questions raised were reasonable and fair'. No one seemed to consider it appropriate for her to ask about the evidence for what was being taught about ancient history.[27]

Therefore she had to wait for a public occasion, which came in February 1993 when Dr Yosef A.A. ben-Jochannan gave the Martin Luther King memorial lecture at Wellesley. He was introduced by the president of Wellesley as a 'distinguished Egyptologist', but as a result of her researches Lefkowitz was aware that he was not what scholars would call an Egyptologist – a scholar of Egyptian language and civilization – but an Afrocentrist who had written many books 'describing how Greek civilization was stolen from Africa, how Aristotle robbed the library of Alexandria, and how the true Jews are Africans like himself'. When he rehearsed these assertions again in his lecture, Lefkowitz

> asked him during the question period why he said that Aristotle had come to Egypt with Alexander, and had stolen his philosophy from the Library at Alexandria, when that Library had only been built after his

death. Dr ben-Jochannan was unable to answer the question, and said that he resented the tone of the enquiry. Several students came up to me after the lecture and accused me of racism, suggesting that I had been brainwashed by white historians.[28]

This was disturbing enough, but the silence of many of her colleagues was perhaps more so, as was the assertion of the dean of her college that 'each of us had a different but equally valid view of history'.[29] What is behind all this – calling myth 'Egyptology', silence, disapprobation, different but equally valid history? It's partly the current intellectual climate, Lefkowitz explains: 'There is a current tendency, at least among academics, to regard history as a form of fiction that can and should be written differently by each nation or ethnic group.'[30]

Mary Lefkowitz is not alone in her experience of the effects of Afrocentric thinking. Norman Levitt, for example, author with Paul Gross of *Higher Superstition: The Academic Left and its Quarrels with Science*, relates the following story:

> I was invited to take part in a course that was essentially a morale building exercise singing the praises of multiculturalism. The course supervisors were well-meaning, but when I mentioned to the class that the Egyptians weren't particularly black, there were cries of outrage from the black students. They had been told that the Egyptians were a great black civilisation. This is actually part of the standard line in the Afrocentric worldview. The belief is that Europeans had come over via the Mediterranean and stolen everything in Western civilisation from the black world, principally, as they suppose, Egypt. I'm a great admirer of the Egyptians myself, but some of the claims which are made on their behalf are just nonsensical.
>
> The trouble is that there has been a great deal of indoctrination around this view of history. And a lot of people have believed it. We're talking here about eighteen or nineteen year old kids from poor educational backgrounds, and they just weren't used to thinking critically about evidence and argument. I tried to talk to this particular class about the use of steel technology in West Africa, which happened in the third or fourth

century BC, and which was actually very impressive. But the black kids wouldn't listen. Once I'd said that the Egyptians had very little to do with black West Africa, they were horrified and outraged, and that was that.[31]

The reaction which Lefkowitz and Levitt encountered amongst students is perhaps not surprising. The students were, after all, young, and, as Levitt says, not used to thinking critically. But that's the problem. They're not used to thinking critically, so they need to get used to it: they need to be taught to do so, and then given lots of practice so that they can go on doing so. But if the faculty and the administration are not only not doing that teaching (and modelling) themselves, but also trying to discourage scholars like Lefkowitz from doing so, how, when, and where are the students ever going to learn?

The general need for critical thinking, and a citizenry that is used to it, is surely obvious enough. It is not as if we inhabit a world where no one ever tries to lie to us, to manipulate, deceive, and persuade us; it's not as if we have no need to evaluate claims, look for evidence, detect rhetorical appeals. Even when it comes to consoling or pride-enhancing mythic history: people who tell stories about history are not always going to do so for good or benevolent reasons. As Lefkowitz points out, history-without-facts may well lead us straight back to the fictive history which served the Third Reich so well. If there are no historical facts, then it is not possible to reject Holocaust denial on the grounds that it doesn't fit with what we know about Nazi Germany.

The historian Richard Evans, who knows quite a bit about Holocaust denial, enough to be called as an expert witness in the David Irving libel trial, puts it this way:

> If history really is nothing more than propaganda, then there's nothing to say it has to be left-wing propaganda, it can just as easily be right-wing propaganda, or racist propaganda, or neo-fascist propaganda ... If we don't believe it's possible to distinguish between truth and falsehood, then we have no means of exposing racism, antisemitism, and neo-

fascism as doctrines of hate built on an edifice of lies, indeed we have no real means of discrediting them at all. We can say of course that we disapprove of them in moral and political terms, but neo-fascists can just put forward opposing moral and political arguments of their own in response, and in the end there are no objective criteria by which we can choose between the two positions.[32]

Epistemic charity

India is one location where exactly this unintended consequence is taking place, as Meera Nanda details in her book *Prophets Facing Backward*. Nanda is a biochemist who left the lab to become involved in the people's science movement in India. Science for her was a liberation from the traditions and narrow opportunities available to most provincial women. When she moved to the USA and went for a second PhD, in philosophy of science, she was shocked to find herself 'drowning in platitudes about cultivating the "alternative sciences" of women, non-Western peoples, and other "victims" of the modern age'.[33] The situation she confronted was rich in ironies: benevolent 'friends' of Third World people helping the reactionary, the rich and the powerful fasten the chains more firmly on women, lower castes, and secularists in India. Intellectuals, 'in their despair over the world they find themselves in, have helped deliver the people they profess to love – the non-Western masses, the presumed victims of "Western science" and modernity – to the growing forces of hatred, fascism, and religious fanaticism'.[34]

The idea behind this unhappy situation is the same sort of all-too-easy fantasy we saw in Marxism. As the vision of a future without conflict rests on the claim that strife will vanish from social relations once material conditions are altered, so a kind of postmodern, postcolonialist hybrid imagines the world will become oppression-free once science and 'Western ways of knowing' have been expelled from the garden.

Much of this thinking is rooted in an understandable opposition to colonialism. It takes the form of a blanket disavowal of 'Western' categories of thought – of science, modernity, the Enlightenment and its project, logic, empiricism, positivism, rationality, universalism and secularism – along with a parallel avowal of categories which are taken to be non-Western: spirituality, folk medicine, tradition, animism and community.

But, of course, this pattern of disavowal and avowal is replete with wishful thinking. It is one thing to say that people should not be oppressed and exploited; it is quite another to claim that the 'ways of knowing' of the oppressed and the exploited are privileged in some systematic way. Not least, the oppressed and exploited are not a solid undifferentiated mass, nor are they a unified univocal group every member of which has identical interests with every other. The reality is that it is perfectly possible, and in fact common, for people to be oppressed in one direction by one set of people, and oppressors in others. Colonized people may be universally oppressed by colonial authorities, but that hardly means that there is no oppression within the colonized society itself. With or without the colonial overlords, there are rich and poor, bosses and workers, men and women, and religious, ethnic and caste discrimination. Sometimes the oppressive colonialists attempt to eliminate some forms of internal oppression, as with the British edicts against *sati* in India; in such cases it is not self-evident that home-grown oppression is invariably better than foreign oppression. This oddly inattentive notion that members of groups can usefully be thought of as essentially identical interchangeable units, integers of colonial oppression, is exactly parallel to Sandra Harding's talk of scientists as rich white straight men that we noticed in Chapter 3. There are rich powerful upper-caste male colonials as well as poor powerless lower-caste women, and all sorts of intermediate modifiers as well.

Further, there is no good reason to think that people who are victimized, who live impoverished lives, will turn out to be any better – morally or otherwise – than other people. The events in Beslan bring this fact into sharp relief. It is generally accepted that the Russian military have behaved very badly in Chechnya; that the Chechen people have suffered enormously. But the Beslan massacre was not the act of a group of people who have come to nobility in their suffering. It rather looks very much more like the act of a group of people who in their immiseration have lost sight of the value of human life.

There is also no evidence that being marginalized or down-trodden improves people's epistemic functioning; that is, their ability to find out the truth about the world. It is true that victims know more about the *experience* of being victims than non-victims do, and this may be useful political and moral knowledge. But there is no reason to think that they therefore know more about the methods which are likely to lead to reliable knowledge. Indeed, there are good reasons for supposing that they will know less about such methods. Not least, by very dint of their marginalization it is likely that they will not have had access to the kind of education and information which will enable them to make real choices between different ways of getting at the truth about the world.

This can be seen in disputes over the difference between myth and history. These include, for example, the push for creation science or 'Intelligent Design' in the USA,[35] the 'saffronization'[36] of history by Hindutva in India,[37] and many of the disputes over repatriation of archaeological remains in Australia, Europe, Canada and the USA.

Kennewick Man is a notorious example of the repatriation disputes. When human skeletal remains were discovered in Kennewick, Washington, in July 1996,[38] the police and coroner thought they belonged to a murder victim and sent them to forensic anthropologist James Chatters. He did indeed find a weapon embedded in Kennewick Man: an ancient stone spear-point. Carbon-dating revealed the bones to be 9,000 years old.[39]

Chatters and other scientists wanted to study the remains, which would provide a wealth of new knowledge about the early inhabitants of the Americas. Unfortunately for that project, local

Native American tribes claimed the remains under the North American Graves Protection and Repatriation Act, known as NAGPRA. Eight scientists sued for the right to study the bones, and the issue has been in the courts ever since, while Kennewick Man is held for safekeeping in the Burke Museum in Seattle. At the time of writing, the decisions have gone in favour of returning Kennewick Man to scientists for study, and the tribes have decided not to appeal the case to the US Supreme Court. But the US Justice Department is still setting limits to what the scientists can do with the bones. It has said it will not permit any chemical or invasive testing on the bones. This edict would prevent further DNA testing.[40]

Given that the bones are 9,000 years old, scientists consider it impossible to be sure there is any close relationship between Kennewick Man and the tribes who live in the region now. NAGPRA was written to protect immediate ancestors, but claims under the law have gone much further than this, citing myths and oral histories for continuity of relationship extending indefinitely into the past. A statement by the president of Friends of America's Past to the NAGPRA Review Committee in May 2001 is clear about this:

> Your obligation is to work within the requirements of the Constitution, and to keep in mind that you are a secular advisory committee. You can not give preference to a group's religious beliefs over other views. Nor may you set aside the law in favour of religious beliefs … [Y]ou may not accept the use of actual religious beliefs as proof of anything. In plain English, if you use religious beliefs to make secular recommendations, the decisions resulting from your recommendations are vulnerable to challenge for violating the First Amendment.[41]

The claims of the Native American tribes were based precisely on linking religious stories with historical events, as the well-known statement by Armand Minthorn of the Umatilla tribe makes plain:

> If this individual is truly over 9,000 years old, that only substantiates our belief that he is Native American. From our oral histories, we know that our people have been part of this land since the beginning of time. We do

not believe that our people migrated here from another continent, as the scientists do ... Some scientists say that if this individual is not studied further, we, as Indians, will be destroying evidence of our own history. We already know our history. It is passed on to us through our elders and through our religious practices.[42]

This kind of argument is antithetical to the tenor of scientific and rational enquiry. It offers no evidence or argument, and it brooks no disagreement or revision. Ironically enough, it may be this very arbitrary quality that endears it to people who are committed to the value of epistemic charity and different ways of knowing. It is 'faith' or belief, a myth or story or narrative; evidence and argument are beside the point. It is a popular postmodernist trope that everything is narrative, everything is a story, an idea that certainly comes in handy when evidence and argument are lacking. It seems more respectable simply to defer to a myth than it is to turn a blind eye to lack of evidence and fallacious argument.

But treating myth as history and history as myth entails denying there are better and worse descriptions of the world. If you're committed to the notion of epistemic egalitarianism, then you have no grounds to distinguish between myth and reality, between the truth according to one's community and the truth *tout court*. There is a huge cost to sanctifying local and situated knowledges in this fashion. It is limiting and constraining. It takes away the freedom to think, question, judge, enquire, investigate, doubt, and to distinguish between consoling fictions and truth. It is not self-evident, for example, that one should allow an accident of birth, whether it be one's race, gender, locality, or religion, to determine, without further reflection, how one goes about finding things out about the world.

In this sense, identity politics is the opposite of progressive or liberating politics. It privileges the unchosen, the happenstance and the biological over the learned, the acquired and the new. There is an irony here. It used to be a vision of the Left that politics was about freeing people from shackles which had been arbitrarily imposed on them by dint of their birth. The early socialist movements in both the

UK and the USA placed great emphasis on the importance of education and self-improvement. There was the vision of freeing everyone; of allowing them to change, to develop their talents and interests, and to become something new. It was not an individualist, selfish dream, of leaving the powerless and oppressed behind; it was a dream of *everyone* being able to escape. Meera Nanda expresses it thus:

> Having grown up in a provincial town in Northern India, I considered my education in science a source of personal enlightenment. Natural science, especially molecular biology, had given me a whole different perspective on the underlying cosmology of the religious and cultural traditions I was raised in. Science gave me good reasons to say a principled 'No!' to many of my inherited beliefs about God, nature, women, duties and rights, purity and pollution, social status, and my relationship with my fellow citizens. I had discovered my individuality, and found the courage to assert the right to fulfil my own destiny, because I learned to demand good reasons for the demands that were put on me.[43]

But for many people on the Left, the dream seems to have been rejected. It is somehow too entangled with the Enlightenment project, too modernist, too 'Western'. For some reason Western intellectuals, and many non-Western too, have decided that people in the Third World do not want or like freedom or change, that 'authentic' Third World people prefer ancient communal ties and oneness with the earth. They tell them to be what they were born, and stay what they were born, on pain of being accused of inauthenticity and mental colonization.

It is a strangely regressive, limiting and limited view that thinks it is somehow progressive to spurn that dream as too Eurocentric or modernist or individualistic. Organic traditional cultures were Burke's idea of a good thing, but they were not Tom Paine's, and it is odd to see the Left choosing Burke over Paine.

7 Institutions, Academe and Truth

Scientific research goes on in particular institutions. Institutions have their own interests and goals, not all of which are necessarily disinterested, or purely epistemic, or in harmony with those of pure research or curiosity-driven science. Goals and interests are a major source of bias in any form of enquiry: knowing what one wants to find in advance tends to shape what one searches for and what one overlooks. It is a claim of many of the critics of science that optimists and Old Deferentialists make too little of the way institutional biases can taint scientific research. There is certainly some truth in this claim. In particular, where corporate interests intersect with scientific practice, then objectivity can very quickly go to the wall. This is easy to demonstrate; consider, for example, the case of the tobacco company Philip Morris and its 'Project Whitecoat'.

The details of Project Whitecoat came to light when the settlement of a 1998 Minnesota court case compelled tobacco companies to make some 32 million pages of their internal documents available to the public.[1] The documents show that in February 1988 a meeting at the UK headquarters of Philip Morris brought together representatives from many of the world's leading tobacco companies. In a note to her bosses about the meeting, Dr Sharon Boyse, a senior scientific adviser at British American Tobacco, set down some of the details of PM's strategy for dealing with the issue of environmental tobacco smoke (ETS), as it was outlined by Helmut Gaisch, their director of science and technology in Europe.

The company was proposing to set up a team of scientists in order to keep the controversy about passive smoking alive; that is, it wanted to ensure that it did not become established scientific fact that there was a link between passive smoking and illness. Boyse revealed that PM's proposed strategy for recruiting scientific consultants for Project Whitecoat was not fully transparent. On a first approach, recruiters would not mention tobacco to potential consultants, they would simply ask the scientists if they were interested in issues to do with indoor air quality. Recruiters would obtain a curriculum vitae from consultants who answered yes; this would enable the company to filter out 'anti-smokers' and those with 'unsuitable backgrounds'.

If scientists elected to join the Philip Morris payroll, then they would be expected 'to operate within the confines of decisions taken by PM scientists to determine the general direction of research, which would ... then be filtered by lawyers to eliminate areas of sensitivity.'[2] Project Whitecoat moved ahead quickly after this initial meeting. Two years later, a report prepared by corporate lawyers Covington and Burling noted that the consultancy programme in the EEC region was 'particularly vigorous and successful': 'We are convinced that it provides greater expertise, more spokesmen, more genuine scientific competence, greater flexibility, and better overall value for money than any other programme.'[3]

A number of specific areas of success were identified:[4]

- PM consultants were major players in international conferences in countries including Canada, Germany, Hungary and Italy.
- Media activities included television and radio interviews, op-ed articles, and numerous media briefings.
- A 'learned society' had been formed – Indoor Air International – which would be 'a major vehicle for reaching a variety of different audiences on IAQ issues'.
- A consultant on the editorial board of the *Lancet* was 'continuing to publish numerous reviews, editorials and comments on ETS and other issues'.[5]

- A consultant – later identified as Roger Perry of Imperial College – was acting as an adviser to a 'particularly relevant committee of the House of Commons'.

- There were hopes that a number of research projects would put the risks associated with ETS 'into perspective', including, for example, work which explored the link between bird-keeping and lung cancer – 'a far more serious factor than anyone has ever alleged ETS to be'.

Project Whitecoat continued until the mid 1990s, after which, according to PM, it was abandoned; however, this was not the extent of the company's, or indeed the wider tobacco industry's, attempts to influence the science of passive smoking. In an article in the *Lancet*,[6] Elisa Ong and Stanton Glantz, from the Institute for Health Policy Studies at the University of California, showed how Philip Morris spent some $4 million in an effort to undermine a major European study, conducted by the International Agency for Research on Cancer (IARC), a research branch of the World Health Organization, into the effects of ETS.

Philip Morris executives were worried that if the IARC study showed passive smoking to be a clear risk factor in the development of cancer, then it would become impossible to resist moves in Europe towards the kind of smoke-free environments legislation which had already been implemented in the USA. Rather than await its publication, then, they decided that a pre-emptive strategy was required, the objectives of which were to delay the progress and/or publication of the study; to affect the wording of its conclusion and official statement of results; to neutralize possible negative results of the study; and to counteract the potential impact of the study on government policy and public opinion.[7]

Ong and Glantz identified a number of ways in which this strategy was implemented: the tobacco industry used consultants to find out as much as possible about the IARC study, so that its weaknesses could be identified in advance of its publication; attempts were made to get the industry's Center for Indoor Air Research (CIAR) involved in the study; the industry sponsored research and publications which showed that passive smoking posed no significant health threats; and a sophisticated public relations campaign was mounted – including a move to establish a 'sound science' organization in Europe – with the aim of keeping the industry's perspective in the minds of politicians, journalists and the general public.

The IARC report was eventually published in October 1998 in the *Journal of the National Cancer Institute*. It showed a 16 per cent increase in risk of lung cancer for non-smokers exposed to the cigarette smoke of a spouse; this was consistent with earlier studies, and led to an editorial in the journal which said that the inescapable conclusion was that 'ETS is a low-level carcinogen'. However, the study did not show this risk at a 95 per cent confidence level, which gave the tobacco industry the opening it needed. Even before the IARC study was published, an article had appeared in the *Sunday Telegraph* in March 1998, probably as the result of media briefings, this time by British American Tobacco, which suggested that a major WHO study had been withheld because it failed to show that passive smoking was a risk factor for lung cancer. And after the IARC study was published, the tobacco industry misrepresented its results as showing that there were no risks associated with ETS, rather than as showing that the risks observed had not reached statistical significance. Ong and Stanton thus concluded that: 'Scientists and policy makers need to understand that they function in an environment that is heavily influenced by covert tobacco industry efforts to subvert the normal decision-making processes.'[8]

It is worth pointing out that the mere fact that the tobacco industry sought to influence the science of passive smoking does not, *in and of itself*, invalidate the claim that the harmful effects of second-hand smoke have been exaggerated. Indeed, one of the interesting things about the PM documents is that they appear to indicate that at least some industry insiders genuinely believed the science which shows passive smoking to be harmful is flawed. Statements such as the following look like (and may well be) the sort of judgement about evidence or its absence that is routine in scientific disagreement: 'Environmental tobacco smoke ... has been claimed to be a hazard to the health of nonsmokers. Although the scientific evidence does not support such a claim, many people believe ETS does cause disease.'[9] And a letter from PM lawyers Covington and Burling to their client includes the following:

> Our preliminary agenda for the meeting ... should leave ample opportunity to discuss ETS as a public affair as well as a scientific issue – and to begin discussion of the role that consulting scientists can play in promoting an objective understanding of the issue among members of the scientific community, government officials and members of the public.[10]

If it is true that industry insiders, including those scientists on the payrolls of the tobacco companies, often genuinely believe that environmental tobacco smoke causes no significant health problems, it raises a whole series of interesting questions about the causes of this belief. Perhaps the belief is justified by the evidence; maybe the tobacco companies have a point when they claim that they are the victims of a concerted campaign on the part of anti-smokers. Or possibly it is an example of the kind of wishful thinking we talked about in the previous chapter; maybe there is an unconscious desire to avoid the cognitive dissonance that might result from thinking one is working for a company whose product is dangerous even to people who do not use it. Or perhaps there is a story to tell about libertarian politics, and an aversion to the idea that it is possible, or even desirable, to create a risk-free world.

The truth of this matter is certainly going to be complex; however, what is clear is that the strong association between tobacco industry affiliation and the view that the scientific evidence fails to show the harm of passive smoking means that claims of scientific objectivity on the part of scientists funded by the tobacco industry must be treated with extreme caution. Deborah Barnes and Lisa Bero, for example, in an analysis of review articles on the effects of passive smoking, found that article conclusions were strongly linked to the affiliations of their authors.[11] Of the 106 articles which they looked at, all published between 1980 and 1995, 37 per cent came down against the view that passive smoking is a health risk; 74 per cent of these were written by people with connections with the tobacco industry. This is 88 times the number which is to be expected by chance. Barnes and Bero claim that their results might well be generalizable:

> ... the conclusions of a review article may be suspect whenever the author has a financial interest in the outcome of the review. Therefore, our findings suggest that the authors of review articles should disclose their affiliations, sources of funding, and other potential financial conflicts of interest, and that the readers of review articles should consider these disclosures when deciding how to judge an article's conclusions.[12]

If the attempt of the tobacco industry to affect the science of passive smoking is the clearest contemporary example of institutional pressures influencing scientific practice, it certainly isn't the only example. Just in the recent past, for example, the sugar industry sought to put pressure on the WHO to scrap guidelines which stated that no more than 10 per cent of a healthy diet should be made up of sugar;[13] and more than half the respondents to a survey of the scientists in the United States Fish and Wildlife Service cited cases where 'commercial interests have inappropriately induced the reversal or withdrawal of scientific conclusions or decisions through political intervention'.[14]

Many scientists are worried by this meshing of political/corporate interests and scientific practice. Sir Martin Rees, for example, recognizes that industry and commerce play an important role in science, but thinks that 'there is the risk that it will be at the cost of the great social benefit of having a cadre of experts who are trusted and are seen as being impartial; and that is a real problem.'[15]

Similarly, Norman Levitt notes that this problem is a function of the way in which institutional science functions:

> In the United States, there is enormous commercial pressure, and where there are working agreements between private corporations and university researchers, things can get badly skewed. For example, there has been a lot of corporate machination to shut researchers up using little known by-ways of American law. And this is a real danger.[16]

Clearly, then, critics of science are right when they say that scientific research is sometimes tainted by biases which are introduced as a result of institutional pressures. However, it is also worth noting that science is not the only discipline which is affected in this way: institutional pressures also have an effect on the humanities and social sciences. This, of course, is well known. Thus, for example, we noted in the previous chapter the difficulties which Mary Lefkowitz and Norman Levitt experienced within their colleges when dealing with the consequences of the institutional protection afforded to Afrocentric modes of thought.

But consider also some of the events which have been played out in recent years at Brigham Young University (BYU), which has its main campus in Provo, Utah. BYU, founded in 1875 by members of the Church of Jesus Christ of Latter-day Saints (LDS) – that is, by Mormons – is an explicitly religious institution. Its mission statement makes it clear that it exists in order to enrich its students – as it sees it – in the Mormon faith:

> The founding charge of BYU is to teach every subject with the Spirit. It is not intended 'that all of the faculty should be categorically teaching religion constantly in their classes, but ... that every ... teacher in this institution would keep his subject matter bathed in the light and colour of the restored gospel'.[17]

It is more than a little difficult to imagine quite what this means when it comes to subjects such as accountancy and computer engineering. But it is immediately clear that BYU, and indeed other colleges and universities which are founded on religious precepts, differ significantly from their secular cousins. No doubt it is tempting to suppose that this difference necessarily undermines any claim which such institutions make that education and research are about the pursuit of truth. However, this would be to oversimplify; it is quite possible for people to carry out perfectly respectable research, in certain delimited fields, even if they believe that the moon is made of semi-skimmed yogurt and that a giant pumpkin is God. Religious institutions don't throw truth out of the window altogether. Their policy is more selective; they keep the bits they like and discard those they don't.

Faculty at BYU are aware that their academic freedom is limited in quite specific ways. The BYU policy on academic freedom is set out in a document which was approved by the university's trustees in September 1992.[18] It is based on a distinction between 'Individual Academic Freedom', which refers to the 'freedom of the individual faculty member "to teach and research without interference," to ask hard questions, to subject answers to rigorous examination, and to engage in scholarship and creative work'; and 'Institutional Academic Freedom', which holds that it is 'the privilege of universities to pursue their distinctive missions'. Bringing these two things together leads BYU to its policy on academic freedom:

> It follows that the exercise of individual and institutional academic freedom must be a matter of reasonable limitations. In general, at BYU a limitation is reasonable when the faculty behaviour or expression *seriously and adversely affects* the university mission or the Church.[19]

The policy document offers three examples of the kinds of things which staff aren't permitted to say to students or in public: (1) something which contradicts or opposes LDS Church doctrine or policy; (2) something which deliberately derides or attacks the LDS Church or its leaders; and (3) something which violates the 'Honor Code'.[20]

It's obvious that such a policy is bound to result in problems.

Scholars working in the humanities or the social sciences are very likely to be enquiring into subjects that could bring them into conflict with the specified limitations on academic freedom. This is especially the case since the limitations are vague enough so that what the BYU authorities consider to be a violation might vary over time, and from case to case, and that faculty might not be clear anyway that particular views or activities are unacceptable.

It is important to make it clear here that there is no evidence that BYU staff are dissatisfied either with the university's strongly religious nature, or with the fact that their academic freedom is necessarily limited. This is not surprising: some 95 per cent of faculty are members of the LDS Church, and also, as a condition of their employment, 'temple-worthy' – a status attained by only about one in five Mormons. The problems have arisen rather because of the perception that the specified limitations on academic freedom are applied with too much zeal; in particular, there is the suspicion that the policy on academic freedom is used in order to silence viewpoints which are unorthodox only on the strictest interpretation of Church doctrine, even though this is not justified by the letter of the policy. This point is perhaps best illustrated by the case of Gail Hurley Houston, who between 1990 and 1996 was an Assistant Professor in the Department of English at BYU.

Professor Houston's story is quite complicated. Indeed, it is the subject of a 62-page report by BYU administrators, which itself was the result of an investigation by the American Association of University Professors, which for its part culminated in an 18-page report.[21] The essence of the story, though, is that Professor Houston's application for tenure (which went forward, as is standard, as she approached her sixth year of employment at BYU) was denied, despite its being supported by her departmental colleagues, her departmental chair, and two of the three requisite tenure committees. It was rejected at the last stage in the tenure process by the University Faculty Council on Rank and Status; the decision to deny tenure was then confirmed by an appeal panel hearing in August 1996.

Houston's application for tenure was not denied on the grounds of the quality of her scholarship. It was denied because in the eyes of the BYU administration she had engaged in 'a pattern of publicly contradicting fundamental Church doctrine and deliberately attacking the Church'.[22] Thus, she was informed that the negative recommendation was because of

> the number and severity of occasions when your actions and words on and off campus … were perceived as harmful to the tenets held by the Church and the university. We feel that not only have these activities failed to strengthen the moral vigour of the university, they have enervated its very fibre.[23]

The BYU administration identified a number of specific occasions where they thought her behaviour had transgressed the boundaries set out in the policy on academic freedom. Perhaps most significant were two instances where she suggested that it is appropriate for Mormons to pray to the 'Heavenly Mother' as well as to the 'Heavenly Father'. The BYU authorities pointed out that she had previously had a warning that such conduct was a clear violation of Church doctrine, and therefore that it was unacceptable, but that she had subsequently repeated the offence. There were also concerns that she had publicly advocated extending the priesthood to women, again in clear violation of Church doctrine.

It would be easy to dismiss these worries on the grounds that they are a function of a deeply ingrained sexism which is characteristic of the Mormon religion. However, while this is probably true, it nevertheless isn't clear that the BYU administrators behaved in quite the arbitrary manner that some commentators have supposed. In other words, there is at least an argument that both the following things are true: Professor Houston was the victim of religious intolerance rooted in a sexist theology; and the BYU administrators correctly applied the terms of their policy on academic freedom.

There is an interesting point here, linked to some of the themes we explored in Chapter 5, about how tempting it is to assess this kind of dispute in terms of viewpoints which are rooted in prior political and ideological commitments. Thus, for example, it would be easy for the authors of this book, in line with their atheism, to declare an anathema on BYU, its arguments and works; that is, to decide in advance that the justification it offered for denying tenure to a feminist scholar was necessarily going to be flawed. But if you look closely at the arguments involved in the issue, the matter is not as straightforward as that.

Consider, for example, the issue of Houston's prayers to a 'Heavenly Mother'. The report of the AAUP found that BYU had not made their case on this issue, because Professor Houston's statements about her visions of a Mother in Heaven were a 'description of a personal vision', and did not constitute public advocacy of belief as the administration charged.[24]

This is pure sophistry. BYU's addendum to the AAUP document was right when it said:

> The AAUP's argument that Professor Houston did not 'advocate' praying to Heavenly Mother is specious. She publicly announced that she engages in the practice of praying to Heavenly Mother and described what a wonderful experience it is. She even described what Heavenly Father and Heavenly Mother say to her in such prayers ... The clear message of her public statements was that it is appropriate to pray to Heavenly Mother, that it is a wonderful experience, and that Heavenly Father and Heavenly Mother accept and respond to such prayers.[25]

However – and it is an important however – the fact that it is at least arguable that BYU acted within the terms of its own policy on academic freedom in the case of Professor Houston, albeit on the basis of the strictest interpretation of that policy, does not mean that there is no institutional pressure at BYU on faculty. The evidence is that there is institutional pressure; that a significant minority of academics fear precisely that they will fall foul of a strict interpretation of the policy on academic freedom; and, in particular, that feminist scholars tend to attract the often unwelcome attention of the BYU authorities.

Thus, for example, the AAUP described a visit to the BYU campus at Provo as follows:

> Many faculty members shared in some detail the narratives of their problems with academic freedom, reappointment, promotion, and tenure, frequently producing documents but asking that their names and identifying circumstances not be included in this report. At least two cases are in litigation against the university. Some cases involve issues of personal conduct that are under investigation and others focus on academic research that raises concern with the administration. Several creative artists in different fields told of pressures to alter works to meet unclear administrative agendas ... Numerous women, some in groups and some alone, spoke to the investigating committee about the hostile climate for women on campus.[26]

Reading this, though, one is led to wonder quite what they expected. Religious doctrine is *always* contested; therefore, disputes about academic freedom are inevitable given the existence of a policy which prohibits overt doctrinal heterodoxy. But it must be said that for a professor at a religious university to complain about this situation is a little bizarre. It comes with the territory. If you're working within the confines of a revealed truth, then there's a lot you can't say. Indeed, with regard to BYU's antipathy towards certain kinds of feminism, it is not unreasonable to ask, though it certainly isn't politic, what exactly feminist scholars think they are doing working there in the first place? After all, the LDS Church is hardly covered in glory when it comes to its record on the rights of women.

The situation at Brigham Young University, then, is fundamentally about religion, and the pressure which the requirement for doctrinal orthodoxy, both in words and practice, exerts upon the faculty. Religion and the pursuit of knowledge, even a religiously circum-scribed 'knowledge', are uneasy bedfellows, so it is entirely to be expected that the university faculty and administration get along with each other only uneasily.

But, of course, religion isn't the only source of tension between a university's administration and academic staff. Consider, for example, the recent and strange goings-on at Columbia University. In March 2005, Columbia released an Ad Hoc Grievance Committee Report on accusations which had been made against faculty members of the Middle Eastern Studies department. The first had come from student Deena Shanker:

> Professor Massad was discussing Israeli incursions into the West Bank and Gaza ... I raised my hand and asked if it was true that Israel sometimes gives warning before bombing certain areas and buildings so that people could get out and no one would get hurt. At this, Professor Massad blew up, yelling, 'If you're going to deny the atrocities being committed against Palestinians, then you can get out of my classroom!'[27]

The committee found that it was 'credible that Professor Massad became angered at a question that he understood to countenance Israeli conduct of which he disapproved, and that he responded heatedly'. In doing so, he 'exceeded commonly accepted bounds by conveying that her question merited harsh public criticism'.[28]

The second accusation had also been levelled against Massad. Tomy Schoenfeld, a one-time student of the General Studies school at Columbia, had reported the following incident:

> I raised my hand to ask a question, and presented myself as an Israeli student. Professor Massad, in his response, asked me whether I served in the Israeli Military, to which I replied I had been a soldier. Then, to my surprise, Professor Massad asked me, 'Well, if you served in the military, then why don't you tell us how many Palestinians have you killed?' I replied by saying that I did not see the relevance of that question to the discussion. Professor Massad, however, insisted, and asked again, 'How many Palestinians have you killed?' I did not answer his question, and remained silent.[29]

In this instance, the committee reached a more nuanced judgement. It found that although there was evidence that an exchange of this nature took place, it was hard to judge its seriousness: 'It appears that this incident falls into a challenging grey zone, neither in the classroom, where the reported behaviour would not be acceptable, nor in an off-campus political event, where it might fit within a not unfamiliar range of give and take regarding charged issues.'[30] The committee also dealt with a third specific allegation, this time against a Professor George Saliba, but found that the substance of that complaint was unproven. In addition, it looked at a number of more general concerns about the department; thus, on the issue of anti-Semitism, it found 'no evidence of any statements made by the faculty that could reasonably be construed as anti-semitic'; and also no evidence that students had been penalized for their political views.

The response to this report has been predictably polarized. Professor Massad, rejecting the findings of the committee, claims to have been the victim of a three-year campaign of intimidation, which has seen students, faculty, an outside pressure group, and the right-wing press all lined up against him. It is Massad's view that the issue is primarily about academic freedom, and the right to hold and articulate certain political views:

> That the Columbia University administration acted as a collaborator with the witch-hunters instead of defending me and offering itself as a refuge from rightwing McCarthyism has been a cause of grave personal and professional disappointment to me. I am utterly disillusioned with a university administration that treats its faculty with such contempt ... The major goal of the witch-hunters is to destroy the institution of the university in general. I am merely the entry point for their political project. As the university is the last bastion of free-thinking that has not yet fallen under the authority of extreme rightwing forces, it has become their main target.[31]

The critics of the Middle Eastern studies department are similarly disillusioned with Columbia's administrators, but in precisely the opposite direction. They allege that the report was a whitewash, in part because the investigating committee was packed with people who were colleagues of the accused and who were anti-Israel

partisans, and also because it restricted itself to investigating only
three instances of misconduct, when in fact many more had been
reported. Thus, for example, Dr Charles Jacobs, president of The
David Project – the outside pressure group to which Massad refers –
argues that:

> The Dirks Committee simply evades the main issue: how to deal with the
> teaching of lies and propaganda by Arabist professors who so demonise
> Israel that defenders of the Jewish state find themselves in a hostile
> environment in their classes. It achieves this evasion by referring to
> incidents of biased, dishonest teaching in exclusively pedagogical and
> psychological terms. It classes them as 'rhetorically combative' methods or
> as expressions of 'uncongenial views' that – and the issue is reduced to
> this – make some students 'uncomfortable'.[32]

It is almost impossible to know what to make of all this. Indeed, it is a
slightly *Alice-in-Wonderland* experience reading the testimonials
which the various protagonists have written in their own defence.
In more than one place, we learn that Professor Massad, an award-
winning teacher, is much loved by his students, even by the Zionists
amongst them.[33] And we are asked to believe either that the events
at Columbia are part of an orchestrated campaign by right-wing
zealots to undermine academic freedom, or that they are indicative
of the predominance of left-wing, anti-Israel, anti-Semitic professors
inside American academia – or maybe even both these things. There
are some saner voices to be heard on the issue,[34] but they are few
and far between.

The obvious similarity between this issue and the situation at
Brigham Young University is that at least some members of both
academic staffs believe that they are under systematic pressure from
external forces – religious, in the case of BYU, political, in the case of
Columbia – mediated and channelled through the actions of their
respective university administrations. However, there is also a second,
less obvious, similarity about these cases. As we have seen, the claim
of the critics of the Middle Eastern studies department at Columbia is

that faculty propagate a distorted, anti-Israel, pro-Palestinian view of the politics of the Middle East; that there is a sort of intellectual conformity within the department which prevents students from hearing a plurality of views about the Middle East. Clearly, it is possible to make exactly the same kind of criticism of the situation at Brigham Young University. It will be recalled that 95 per cent of BYU faculty are 'temple-worthy' Mormons; and that according to BYU's own policy on academic freedom, professors are not permitted to articulate views which are doctrinally heterodox. Almost inevitably, then, the education which students receive at BYU will be highly circumscribed when compared to their secular equivalent. How, for example, is it possible to take the challenges of Skinner's radical behaviourism seriously if one 'knows' that human freedom is a gift from God? And why would one give any credence to the idea that gender is socially constructed if one believed that femininity is divinely inspired?

There are various permutations of this kind of academic or intellectual conformity. It can be intradepartmental, as, arguably, it is in the Columbia case; intrainstitutional, as in the case of BYU; or intradisciplinary, as would be the case if a particular academic discipline came to be dominated by one specific viewpoint. It can also be more or less rationally justified; thus, for example, Darwinism is overwhelmingly dominant within the biological sciences, but for good evidential reasons. And it also exerts its effects just as strongly on faculty as it does on students. A good way to explore some of these issues is to spend a little time looking at the situation which has existed within the world of literary studies for the last 25 years or so.

David Lehman's 1991 book *Signs of the Times* is a jeremiad about the contemporary state of English and literature departments in the US.[35] Deconstructionist ways of thinking and writing were ascendant; truth was out of fashion; literary critics produced a flood of books which, as Frank Kermode put it, 'few people interested in literature, and not even all professionals, can read'; Clara Claiborne Park noted that Shakespeare, in the name of the death of the author, had become 'Shakespeare'; and to think that literature might have something to say about the human condition was to be committed to a naïve 'metaphysics of presence'. Along with all this, student enrolments on English courses were down, op-eds were appearing in mainstream media decrying the vagaries of intellectual fashion, and academics told each other 'bleakly funny' stories of student ignorance ('the battles of World War Eleven') around dinner tables.[36]

In terms of the concerns of this chapter, the interesting thing about this situation is not so much the issue of the merits or otherwise of deconstruction or 'Theory', but rather the hegemony of Theory within certain parts of the American academy. Lehman quotes Derrida saying that 'America is deconstruction', and describing the USA as 'that historical space which reveals itself as being undeniably the most sensitive, receptive or responsive space of all to the themes and effects of deconstruction'.[37] Lehman also cites the postmodernist feminist Julia Kristeva saying in the mid 1980s that hard-line deconstructionism had achieved a kind of monopoly in the higher echelons of literary criticism.[38] Lehman, for his part, thought that the late twentieth century was 'the age of theory in the seminar rooms of America' and that deconstruction was the 'paradigmatic theory of the age'.[39]

Not surprisingly, Theory's near hegemony in literary and cultural studies has had various important consequences. It has changed the way many subjects are taught, and the status of particular approaches and areas of specialization. This in turn has had an effect on faculty hiring and promotion, and on what gets published in journals and as books, which naturally has changed the rules for what people need to do to succeed.

What this amounts to is that to get ahead in literary studies one has had to play the Theory game. Thus, for example, Lehman recalls being told at a Modern Language Association (MLA) convention, the annual job fair/chatfest for literature scholars, that

> If you want to make it in the criticism racket, you have to be a deconstructionist or a Marxist or a feminist. Otherwise you don't stand a

chance. You're not taken seriously. It doesn't matter what you know or don't know. What counts is your theoretical approach. And this means knowing jargon, and who's in and who's out.[40]

This assessment is echoed by William Kerrigan, who notes that

Graduate students were told that the profession was now the site of the Theory Explosion, and those who did not champion a theory, or at least show themselves 'theory-literate', would not get jobs. One began to hear in tenure cases the argument that appearances at conferences and institutes should be counted as equivalents to publications. Professional dossiers swelled with lists of slide-show presentations, conferences organised, occasions where the visible young professor had served as 'respondent' on panel discussions with titles like 'Getting Licked: Lesbian Exchanges in the Mother Tongue.'[41]

Kerrigan is not exaggerating here about the popularity of, shall we say, surprising titles that accompanied the Theory explosion. Session and paper titles which have graced the annual MLA convention include: 'Jane Austen and the Masturbating Girl'; 'The Muse of Masturbation'; 'Clitoral Imagery and Masturbation in Emily Dickinson'; 'Desublimating the Male Sublime: Autoerotics, Anal Erotics, and Corporeal Violence in Melville and William Burroughs'; and '"The Entree Was Long and Streit, and Gastly for to See": Visual and Verbal Penetration in the Knight's Tale'.

In 2003 *Chronicle of Higher Education*, a weekly publication dealing with American academia, paid tribute to this penchant for the absurd title by establishing an 'Annual Awards for Self-Consciously Provocative MLA Paper Titles' (familiarly called the Provokies), only to abolish them a year later on the grounds that when it came to crafting outrageous titles, convention delegates' hearts were no longer really in it. However, given that the 2004 convention featured papers entitled 'She's Just Like Alvy Singer! Kissing Jessica Stein and the Postethnic Jewish Lesbian' and 'Wandering Genitalia in Late Medieval German Literature and Culture', this assessment was surely premature.

Although it is hard to read this sort of thing without laughing, there are a couple of serious points to be made here. One is that there is at least an argument that oddities of this sort are related to a relentless institutional competitiveness, which requires ambitious scholars to outdo each other in originality – or perceived originality – and provocativeness; and that they must do so in terms of the standards of Theory. Thus, for example, Mark Crispin Miller claims that there is

> an economic basis to the theory craze. The academy's eccentric market system calls for unrelenting publication by untenured faculty, and by the tenured few who want to rise ... That constant economic pressure has necessitated 'theory' as we know it: a dense and ever-shifting bog that offers ample ground for further output (a/k/a 'interventions'), without which you don't have a job, or, in many places, get a decent raise.[42]

The other serious point is that all this has significantly damaged the reputation of literary studies. Every year the MLA convention attracts the scorn of the mainstream media. Thus, for example, a recent article in the *New York Times* claims that the MLA 'has come to resemble a hyperactive child who, having interrupted the grownups' conversation by dancing on the coffee table, can't be made to stop'; and it cites with approval Sanford Pinsker's view that literary studies has become a 'laughing stock', and his fear 'that there are other, even more outrageous would-be celebrities hoping to cash in on whatever post-postmodernism turns out to be'.[43]

There is a school of thought which suggests that deconstruction and Theory are on the wane. Terry Eagleton, for example, in the preface to the second edition of his book *Literary Theory*, suggests that the Paul de Man affair, and the fall of communism, have rather undercut Theory's self-styled radicalism; and certainly books with titles like *Reading after Theory*, and *Life. After. Theory* have begun to appear. However, while there is arguably an element of truth to this – deconstruction specifically no longer dominates the field as it did in the 1980s – it would be easy to exaggerate the extent to which it has occurred. If you doubt Theory's continuing significance, particularly in the USA, just drop in on the next MLA convention; or visit the section of the local university bookstore dedicated to Judith Butler, Gilles Deleuze, Felix Guattari, Luce Irigaray, Gayatri Chakravorti Spivak, Homi Bhabha, and Fredric Jameson; or browse a college catalogue for postcolonial studies, subaltern studies, queer theory, gender studies, whiteness studies, disability studies, critical race theory, critical legal theory. It may be that the *word* 'Theory' doesn't deliver quite the *frisson* it once did, but the thing it stands for hasn't gone away yet.

For our purposes, Theory's hegemony matters because it illustrates where intradisciplinary conformity can end up. In the case of Theory, what has happened is something like the intellectual equivalent of the evolution of the Peacock's tail. As Theory gained a foothold in the academy, it became necessary for ambitious young academics to compete on a terrain which it defined. The more Theory dominated, the fiercer the competition became, which meant that if scholars wanted to be noticed, they had to engage in increasingly ostentatious displays of theoretical virtuosity. In the end, driven by a positive feedback loop, display became everything: the peacocks had colonized the world of literary studies.

It might be tempting to suppose that none of this really matters. After all, scholars have played their academic games for as long as there have been universities, and conformity, in and of itself, is not necessarily a bad thing. So why should we worry? The answer to this question is that we should worry for the kinds of reasons which have motivated the writing of this book. Truth matters; and to the extent that Theory has marginalized the pursuit of truth, whether by denying its existence or burying it in a display of peacockish superfluity, it is to be regretted. But there is also an answer which is more specific to the concerns of this chapter. Intradisciplinary and intra-institutional conformity lead all too easily to a kind of unthinking groupthink. This can be illustrated by considering the bitter row over the alleged mistreatment of the Yanomami Indians of

Venezuela which first engulfed the world of anthropology in the late summer of 2000, and which still rumbles on to this day.

The spark which lit the blue touchpaper was an email sent by anthropologists Terence Turner and Leslie Sponsel to Louise Lamphere, then president of the American Anthropological Association. It warned her of an 'impending scandal', which in 'its scale, ramifications, and sheer criminality and corruption ... is unparalleled in the history of Anthropology'. According to Turner and Sponsel, the scandal would be caused by the publication of Patrick Tierney's *Darkness in El Dorado*, which alleged on the basis of 'convincing evidence' that geneticist James Neel and anthropologist Napoleon Chagnon had greatly exacerbated, and probably started, the epidemic of measles that killed many hundreds of Yanomami in 1968; that their research team had provided no help to the dying tribespeople; that 'in all probability' the epidemic was started deliberately in order to provide scientific support for Neel's eugenicist ideas; and that Chagnon had systematically falsified his research data on the Yanomami.

These claims quickly found their way onto the Internet, where unsurprisingly they caused quite a stir in the anthropological community, before being picked up and publicized by the mainstream media. *The Chronicle of Higher Education* was perhaps the first off the mark with its story, 'Scholars Fear that Alleged Misdeeds by Amazon Anthropologists Will Taint Entire Discipline';[44] and the London *Guardian* wasn't far behind with its take on the issue, headlining it: 'Scientist "killed Amazon Indians to test race theory"'.[45] This all made for great copy; there was only one problem – the allegations against Neel and Chagnon were untrue.

This actually became clear pretty quickly. On 21 September 2000, less than a month after Turner and Sponsel's original email, Susan Lindee, a historian of science at the University of Pennsylvania, having read Neel's entire field-notes for the 1968 work in Venezuela, circulated an open email on the Internet, in which she showed that the specific allegations levelled against Neel and Chagnon were unfounded. Thus, she concluded that it was clear that the measles epidemic 'drastically disrupted' Neel's field research, and 'that he was at times frustrated, even angry, about this situation'.

> A measles outbreak emphatically did not facilitate his research ... I am of course basing the above account on correspondence and field notes in the papers of James V. Neel, and if we wish to adopt an X-files theory of history, we could propose that he planted these records, including the much-scribbled on and often almost illegible field notes, in order to mislead future historians about his actual behaviour in the field.[46]

Lindee's assessment was confirmed by a number of independent enquiries. For example, the American Society of Human Genetics found that

> none of the allegations against Neel stand up against the facts as we have determined them. It saddens and angers us that the reputation of one of the most outstanding human geneticists of the 20th century was threatened ... by a book with numerous misrepresentations and disproved allegations.[47]

And the National Academy of Sciences concluded that Tierney's 'misuse of source material and the factual errors and innuendoes in his book do a grave disservice to a great scientist and to science itself'.[48]

If this were just a tale of a badly researched book, an ill-considered email, and inaccurate reportage, then it would be interesting enough. But there is a whole lot more to it than this, because lurking in the background of these events is a set of issues about anthropology's own self-image.

The best way to understand what this set of issues is about is to know that Neel and Chagnon were proponents of biological and sociobiological explanations of human behaviour. Chagnon had achieved a certain notoriety in the world of anthropology for claiming that aggression and warfare are integral to the culture of the Yanomami, and that this is reflected in their mythology, politics and ceremonial life. Moreover, he claimed to have shown that there is a link between warfare and reproduction; that successful warriors have more sexual partners and children than their less successful counterparts.

As we saw in Chapter 5, when we looked at the events which occurred in the aftermath of the publication of Edward O. Wilson's *Sociobiology*, ideas of this kind are not universally popular. This is especially the case in the world of anthropology, where, for example, in 1983, the American Anthropological Association passed a resolution noting that Derek Freeman's *Margaret Mead and Samoa*, a book which suggested that behaviour has a biological component, had been 'consistently denounced by knowledgeable scholars as being poorly written, unscientific, irresponsible and misleading'. It is unsurprising, then, that Chagnon, in particular, as an anthropologist, had been attacked from within the profession on numerous previous occasions.

Terence Turner, joint author of the email which sparked off the row over Tierney's book, is his most vocal and longstanding critic. In 1994, in the *Chronicle of Higher Education*, Turner was quoted as saying that Chagnon had used 'aspects of the Yanomamo tragedy to dramatise himself on the basis of patently false claims'; and that 'Anthropologists who work with people who really have their backs to the wall … ought to be fighting for them, and not dramatising their own careers.'[49] In January 2000 Turner spoke up again, this time in the *Los Angeles Times Magazine*, claiming that Chagnon's politics 'are bad … His ideas are used by miners and politicians, especially in Brazil, to argue for a breakup of Yanomamo land'; and also that Chagnon's idea that dominant males get more women, and therefore pass on more genes, 'is very close to the Nazi idea that there's a leadership gene that the dominant people pass on and this is the natural order'.[50]

The University of Michigan released an official statement on Tierney's book, which had this to say about Turner:

> Every expert witness we have consulted considers Terence Turner to be
> Chagnon's most passionate adversary. He is perhaps the prototypic
> 'militant, morally engaged' anthropologist, with especially ferocious
> dedication to the rights of threatened indigenous people ... Turner
> appears from his writings to believe virtually every bad thing he has heard
> about Chagnon, whether from the Salesian missionaries ... a disgruntled
> former student of Chagnon's, or Chagnon's professional rivals ... What sets
> Turner apart from Chagnon's other critics is the intensity of his anger,
> which eyewitnesses say included interrupting Chagnon with a tirade
> during the 1994 'truce' session with Father Bortoli.[51]

Although Turner may be the most extreme of Chagnon's critics, his
general views are commonplace in the world of anthropology. The
American Anthropological Association held an 'open-microphone'
session at their November 2000 meeting, long after it was clear that
the major allegations levelled against Neel and Chagnon were false,
to allow people to express their views on the controversy. According
to Thomas Gregor and Daniel Gross, what followed

> was a succession of speakers, many of them with evident hostility toward
> Chagnon. Virtually every aspect of his behaviour, relevant or otherwise,
> was open for public dissection. One participant took the microphone and
> claimed that Chagnon had treated her rudely in the field during the
> 1960s. A colleague from Uganda praised Tierney's book and alleged that
> Westerners manufactured the Ebola virus and disseminated it in his
> country, just as Chagnon and Neel had started the measles epidemic.
> Members of the audience applauded both speakers.[52]

Gregor and Gross suggest that perhaps the most fruitful way to
understand the opprobrium directed towards Neel and Chagnon is
in terms of anthropology's own self-image; that is, in terms of its
desire to exculpate itself from the sins of its own past. They note that
anthropology has always been intertwined with particular moral
commitments. Until the early 1970s, this meant 'a rejection of racism,
respect and support for indigenous peoples, cultural relativism, and
social justice.'[53] However, in recent decades, the moral compass has
shifted, meaning that anthropologists are no longer content merely

to articulate the moral failings of Western society, but rather they have turned their focus towards anthropology itself, developing 'an extended self-critique'. Thus, Gregor and Gross point out that the 1970s saw the publication of many books in which anthropology

> was seen to facilitate colonialism and other repressive relationships ... to contribute to the abuse of indigenous peoples by romanticised descriptions of their culture that failed to take account of their threatened status, and to permit racially and culturally alien outsiders to produce and market false, misleading, and even exploitative caricatures of other societies.[54]

At the same time as this process of self-criticism was becoming established, postmodern approaches began to gain a foothold within the discipline, thereby challenging 'the methodological assumptions associated with rigorous, modern social science inquiry', and requiring new standards for evaluating truth-claims, which are 'likely to be subjective in nature, including, for example, flexibility, sensitivity ... beauty, strength or force'.[55] From the perspective of postmodernism, social science, as a science, is just another mechanism for objectifying and oppressing people, and it is, therefore, to be resisted. In its place, it is necessary to develop an anthropology which is a 'mode of social engagement and advocacy'. Thus, Gregor and Gross note Louise Lamphere's claim that 'engaged anthropology' is vitally important, and that impersonal scientific concerns should always come second to moral commitment.[56]

It is now easy to see how Neel and Chagnon became the victims of an academic witch-hunt. Their kind of anthropology is constitutive of the sins of anthropology's past; their genetic and sociobiological commitments, if not racist, are certainly part of the 'grand narrative' of Western science, which has brought in its train oppression and subjugation; and their preoccupation with violence and aggression functions to preclude the emergence of an 'anthropology of peace',[57] and undermines a political commitment to the idea of the noble savage.

In the name, then, of a morally committed anthropology, Neel and Chagnon were hung out to dry. It is true, of course, that they had their supporters; but, in a culture which, above all else, valorizes engagement, advocacy, activism and commitment, their enemies had the louder voices; certainly, loud enough to ensure that in the early autumn of the year 2000, the world's media were full of stories of fascistic anthropologists, willing to experiment on their fellow human beings. No matter that none of it was true; we live, after all, in a postmodern world, where the message is everything. So if it is necessary to trash the reputations of two of the world's major scholars, in order to demonstrate the political credentials of an engaged anthropology, then so be it. Truth, after all, is subservient to moral and political commitments; so what possible reason can there be for thinking that it mattered?

We've seen that we don't always straightforwardly want the truth. It's not always our first goal or priority; sometimes it's not even on the list. There are many reasons not to want the truth in particular cases, many sources of the temptation to blur or fake or ignore or deny it. The reasons can be personal, political, moral, even cognitive. We may also do both at once – know the truth, and at the same time push it away, hide it, cover it up, make it go out of focus; grasp it cognitively as a fact while not taking it in emotionally. This is a useful coping mechanism, and often an emotional necessity. We do it with trivial matters as well as large ones – true fact X irritates me, therefore I'll ignore X. A beneficial move, in many ways; it can be good for our blood pressure, our mood, our ability to concentrate and work, to decide to withdraw our attention from true facts that make us angry or sad or afraid.

This is not exactly denial; it's more like minimization or compartmentalization, as if true facts all came with a top right corner which one could click to make tiny. It's still there, but it's not filling the screen. Selective attention is a fine thing sometimes.

Unfortunately, it probably also trains us in bad habits, if we're not aware and alert. It may get us used to the idea that truth is subject to human will. If we minimize true facts that we dislike too often, we may lose sight of the fact that it is our reaction and degree of attention that is subject to our wills, and start to think that the facts themselves are subject to our wills. But on the whole they're not.

Facts about our own emotional and mental states, if there are such facts, may be subject to our wills, but facts about the rest of the world are not.

It could be said that everything that is interesting about what it is to be human takes place in this small space: the space between the world as it is in itself, and human understanding of it. The space, that is to say the difference, between true facts, reality, truth, what is Out There, on the one hand, and what we human beings make of that reality, on the other. Our thoughts about it, our curiosity about it. That's only one way of looking at what it is to be human, of course, but it is surely one that has motivated many of the best enquirers. What is the cosmos, what is the mind, can humans understand either or both? There seems to be an enormous mismatch between the universe and its nature, and a bipedal primate that evolved in the thin layer of life on one planet in one microdot of time. To some thinkers that mismatch means we might as well give it up, accept our limitations, and opt for solidarity and social hope rather than a hopeless quixotic quest for truth about the world. To others the mismatch is more in the nature of a challenge or incentive. The fact that we are jumped-up apes in clothes is all the more reason to try to figure out the cosmos this jumped-up ape evolved in. How interesting if natural physical processes produced not only stars and planets and rocks and trees but one animal that can understand the laws of those very processes. What a good reason to try.

In other words, that's one answer to the question, 'Why does truth matter?' It matters because we are the only species we know of that has the ability to find it out. In a way that makes it almost a duty to do so. A duty imposed by no one, for which we don't have to answer – but a kind of duty all the same.

However, not everyone sees the matter that way. It's a human impulse to try to understand and investigate, but it's also a human impulse to try to protect our illusions, or at least a little breathing-room for our illusions; to keep some possibility of optimism, which can often seem to require the kind of blurring or minimization of truth mentioned above. There is a political dimension to this impulse, which we have been considering throughout the book. We have seen that this tendency is far from being a monopoly of the Left; it's essential to religious belief, for one thing, and the more literal and fundamentalist the belief is, the more necessary it is to ignore or deny interfering facts.

But to the extent that the Left is committed to hopes for (some day) improving the intractable social ills that have tormented humans as far back as we can see – inequality, exploitation, injustice, violence – it seems to have a built-in motivation for wanting to be hopeful about the future. People who are less worried about social ills – because they happen elsewhere, to other people, or are better than they used to be, or are necessary for the economy, or are just generally not on the radar – are more willing to think the future will be much like the present only with more electronics. The Left want to think bad arrangements will improve, and soon. It needs or wants optimism about the future.

This can be seen as a grammatical situation. Leftist thinking is future- and conditional-tense thinking, it's about will, and could, might and should. Both of those tenses are where we talk about matters on which decisive final contradiction and refutation are not possible. 'Sure', we are used to saying, more or less sarcastically or mockingly, 'it *could* happen; anything *could* happen.' Just so, and what a consoling thought that can be. But as we saw in Chapter 6, consoling thinking can infect the more clear-eyed, hard-headed kind – and that's where the trouble lies.

It may be – this is highly speculative, be it noted – that this temperamental affinity for the future, which entails a background idea that the latest newest thing is the best thing, brings with it a heightened responsiveness to fashion.

If so, perhaps this would explain the oddity we have been discussing throughout this book: that truth has become unhip, and with researchers of all people. That seems such an unlikely situation – as if mathematics were out of fashion in engineering, or microscopes in biology, or wrenches in plumbing. It seems so basic – such an essential tool of the whole enterprise. If researchers aren't after the truth, surely they might as well hand in their badges and try another line of work. In fact, to put it bluntly, surely it's not so much that they might as well, as that they ought to. If they're not after the truth they have no business being researchers at all. It's a kind of fraud, setting up as a scholar – as someone who engages in research – while disbelieving in the existence or reality of truth.

That thought should apply to any branch of enquiry. It is simply part of the job description, and a very important part at that. Detectives and forensic scientists are supposed to collect evidence in order to find the true perpetrators, not false ones. They are not under orders to plant evidence, or to conceal, tamper with, throw out evidence. The same applies to any other kind of enquiry. Getting things wrong, providing false incorrect inaccurate answers to questions is not the goal. So people with a programmatic, or perhaps temperamental, disbelief in even the possibility of truth, have no business going into any branch of enquiry or pedagogy at all. There are fields where indifference to truth is no handicap – advertising, PR, fashion, lobbying, marketing, entertainment. In fact there are whole large, well-paid, high-status sectors of the economy where truth-scepticism, wishful thinking, fantasy, suspension of disbelief, deletion of the boundary between dreams and reality, are not only not a handicap but essential to the enterprise. Much of capitalism runs on peddling illusions and fantasies, and most of the entertainment industry would be lost without them. We spend a lot of our leisure time staring into a rectangular box, feeding our fantasy habit.

We need our dreams and fantasies, our stories and imaginaries. They're good for us. We need the cognitive rest from the labour of confronting reality all day, we need to be able to imagine alternatives, we need the pleasure of fantasy. But we also need to hang on to awareness of the difference between dreams and reality. It is necessary that the sectors of the economy and culture dedicated to the manufacture of illusions and manipulations be balanced by, and ultimately subordinate to, those dedicated to the other thing. We need illusions but we also decidedly need truth, so we need institutions and people committed to finding it and defending it against the liars, deceivers, tricksters and persuaders.

Such institutions are a turn-off to a lot of people. Understandably. They seem dull, chilly, colourless: work instead of play; school as opposed to break. Making up stories, painting pictures, acting out dramas, are more fun than compiling statistics. Tours of movie studios are more popular than tours of laboratories. So ... sometimes there is an impulse to import a little of the play-world into the reality-based institutions.

This may be one explanation for the apparent anomaly that hyperscepticism about truth is fashionable in some branches of scholarship. At any rate, anomalous or not, the fashion is there.

One could also talk of community norms, rather than fashion. That's a more charitable and perhaps fairer way of looking at the matter, which encompasses the complication that fashion and groupthink, conformity and imitation, are not all bad. Far from it. This is a complication that one sees at work all the time in wrangles over political correctness: yes, sometimes people who see racism hiding under every bed can be tedious or obsessive, but all the same, it is a good thing that racism has gone out of fashion to the extent that it has, and that people feel socially inhibited about avowing racist ideas. The same applies to sexism, homophobia, ethnocentrism and other varieties of formerly disregarded exclusion and cruelty. Ideally, the community norms are based on reasoned argument rather than operant conditioning, but even if the norms are merely habitual and imitative, the effects in the world are preferable to those of worse community norms.

As we have seen, the community norms of truth sceptics are at least partly motivated by some decent, altruistic ideas; perhaps chiefly by a desire to carve out a space for people – sometimes other people to whom the academics want to offer assistance and epistemic backup, sometimes people in general, sometimes the academics themselves – to believe whatever they want to believe without having to answer for it to a committee of bureaucratic, heartless, authoritarian Experts.

Richard Rorty has a related thought in *Contingency, Irony, Solidarity*:

> It is central to the idea of a liberal society that, in respect to words as opposed to ideas, persuasion as opposed to force, anything goes. This openmindedness should not be fostered because, as Scripture teaches, Truth is great and will prevail, nor because, as Milton suggests, Truth will always win in a free and open encounter. It should be fostered for its own sake. *A liberal society is one which is content to call 'true' whatever the upshot of such encounters turns out to be.*[1]

Michael Lynch in his book *True to Life* comments on the passage:

> The argument lurking behind the scenes here is, apparently, quite seductive. While it is unclear whether Rorty himself would ever have endorsed it, I think many people clearly do. It goes like this: liberalism involves equal respect for different conceptions of how to live. The ultimate way of showing respect is to say that every view of the good life is equally true. Therefore, truth can't be understood as independent of people's beliefs. Truth – to use Barry Allen's ringing phrase – is just whatever passes for truth in one's shared community.[2]

Susan Haack roundly argues against this conception of truth:

> 'True' *is* a word we apply to statements about which we agree; but that is because, if we agree that things are thus and so, we agree that it is true that things are thus and so. But we may agree that things are thus and so when it is *not* true that things are thus and so. So 'true' is not a word that truly applies to all or only statements about which we agree; and neither, of course, does calling a statement true mean that it is a statement we agree about.[3]

If Rorty does not mean this, he makes many statements that sound very like it, thus at least misleading the unwary. Haack points out that he is more radical in some sentences than others: 'Rorty doesn't always sound this radical; just very often.'[4] The problem is obvious enough: tolerance and 'openmindedness' are one thing, and truth is another. It is possible, and necessary, to be openminded and tolerant about words and persuasion, without calling them 'true'.

Farther back

In any case, fashion and groupthink are explanations (if they are) rather late in the causal chain. Even if peer pressure, trendiness, the need to fit in and conform and avoid looks of amused contempt and charges of naïveté and cluelessness and pretheoriticality, enforce much conformity now, what caused the fashion to become a fashion in the first place? Was it just a brainwave in the head of Jacques Derrida? Or an accumulation of brainwaves in Nietzsche, Freud, Heidegger, Derrida, Foucault and others that reached critical mass with Derrida's famous lecture at Johns Hopkins in 1966?

Yes, partly. Up to a point, there is no need to look for motivation beyond that – the superstructure will do the job. The ideas did interest and catch the attention of academics, and spread from there, as ideas will. New, fruitful, interesting, provocative ideas, that can be processed into interesting and provocative articles and books and thus into tenure and promotion, are motivation enough. The novelty and provocation are part of the point. As we saw in Chapter 7, under the right conditions, novelty and provocation can be more successful, more publishable and attention-getting, than sober unsurprising ones. To the extent that that is true, there is no longer a question, 'What motivates rational academics to say such anti-rational things?' If rational academics say such things not despite the anti-rationality but because of it, there seems little need to look for deeper motivations. They do it for pragmatic, instrumental, vocational reasons, that's all. It works. It gets them what they want.

And along with that there is perhaps the fact that they can – at least in some departments. That's much less true in some than others, of course. Some sections even of the humanities are decidedly empirically based – history, for example – and there just making it up is frowned on – though there are postmodernist historians who 'problematize' notions of objectivity and evidence. Other sections, such as philosophy, are partial to notions such as noncontradiction, and that too puts a brake on rootless word-spinning. But in less rigorous literature (or, now, 'Theory') depart-ments, and identity-group 'studies' departments, and some branches of social science such as anthropology, there is more freedom (or anarchy, one might prefer to call it). People climb Everest because it's there, and rob banks because that's where the money is, and look for lost items under street lamps because that's where the light is better, and spin complicated but empty pseudo-theories in studies departments because they can get away with it.

Though not always unimpeded, or without a fuss. In 1992, when the English department (not, mark, the Philosophy department) of Cambridge University nominated Jacques Derrida for an honorary degree, philosophers including W.V.O. Quine wrote a letter of protest.

> M. Derrida describes himself as a philosopher, and his writings do indeed bear some marks of writings in that discipline. Their influence, however, has been to a striking degree almost entirely outside philosophy ... In the eyes of philosophers, and certainly those working in leading departments of philosophy throughout the world, M. Derrida's work does not meet accepted standards of clarity and rigor.[5]

And the split continues as sharp as ever. When Derrida died in October 2004, some obituaries, especially that in the *New York Times*, expressed reservations about his philosophical merit. Several admirers of Derrida wrote letters to the *Times* to protest at the lack of unqualified adulation; one letter 'quickly gathered so many signatures that we realised a website was needed to record the names of those who wished to be heard'.[6] So the website was created, and a great many signatures duly appeared, but it is noticeable how small the proportion of philosophers is compared to that of people in literature, arts and related departments. It is also noticeable how readily Derrida's champions resort to an argument from celebrity. Judith Butler for example wrote:

> If Derrida's contributions to philosophy, literary criticism, the theory of painting, communications, ethics, and politics made him into the most internationally renowned European intellectual during these times, it is because of the precision of his thought, the way his thinking always took a brilliant and unanticipated turn, and because of the constant effort to reflect on moral and political responsibility.[7]

This is an interesting sentence. First there is that ambiguous, not to say equivocal, 'If'. It can mean two fairly contradictory things: either something like 'because' or 'since' or 'assuming that', or the more usual meaning of 'if', which leaves it open whether Derrida is in fact 'the most internationally renowned European intellectual during these times' or not. In other words, it is not clear whether Butler is or is not saying that Derrida is 'the most internationally renowned European intellectual' – but even though it is not clear, the sentence leaves the impression that she is, while also leaving an escape clause. If dissenters retort that Derrida is not 'the most internationally renowned European intellectual' Butler can reply that she didn't say he was. To put it another way, Butler both makes a rather outlandish claim about Derrida, and makes it in a sufficiently qualified, hedged, equivocal way that the outlandishness is occluded.

The second, more interesting, point is the *non sequitur*. If Derrida is the most internationally renowned European intellectual, she says, it is 'because of the precision of his thought, the way his thinking always took a brilliant and unanticipated turn, and because of the constant effort to reflect on moral and political responsibility'. But is it? Why does that follow? It doesn't seem to. People – even intellectuals and thinkers – may become 'renowned' for reasons other than the precision of their thought, and having precision of thought is not always or necessarily a path to renown. So why should we believe that the precision of Derrida's thought, the way his thinking always took a brilliant and unanticipated turn, and his constant effort to reflect on moral and political responsibility constitute the reason for his renown?

As a matter of fact why should we not simply conclude that much or most of Derrida's renown is the result of frequent mention by Butler and others like her? That he merely has what in US electioneering and public relations circles is called 'name recognition,' which is well known to be quite independent of merit and quality. Serial murderers have much higher name recognition than any intellectuals, and it's not because of their precision of thought (though it may be because their thinking takes some unanticipated turns). Here the two oddities of that sentence come together. In fact Derrida is not the most internationally renowned European intellectual, and the fact that Butler thinks he may be (don't forget that 'if') is a slightly pathetic reflection of the parochialism of Theory. Derrida, like Butler herself, was a 'superstar' in the particular hermeneutic circles they travel in – but not outside them. Butler has a distorted idea of Derrida's renown because the people she knows talk about him a lot, and she has apparently forgotten that the world of Theory is not coterminous with the entire world of intellectuals.

This is a minor point, of course, but there is something interesting about it all the same; it is interesting as a symptom, if nothing else. The obvious circularity and irrelevance of Butler's argument, and her apparent indifference to them (her letter is there on the site for all to see, so presumably she is happy with it), point to something very worrying about postmodernism. There is a frivolity, a lack of responsibility, an indifference to canons of coherence, logic, rationality and relevance – which are reminiscent not of the Left or progressivism, but, as Richard Wolin argues, of counter-Enlightenment and reaction.

That is not a mere accidental association, it is what counter-Enlightenment and reaction are all about: the rejection of reason, enquiry, logic and evidence, in favour of tradition, religion, instinct, blood and soil, The Nation, The Fatherland. That is the sort of thing that remains standing once canons of coherence and relevance are stripped away. The Left is not well-advised to discredit or undermine reason and respect for truth, because those are ultimately the only tools the Left has against the irrationalist appeals of the Right.

There is a profound irony in the situation – in postmodernist epistemic relativism. It is thought to be, and often touted as, emancipatory. It is supposed to set us all free: free from all those coercive repressive restrictive hegemonic totalizing old ideas. From white male Western reason and science, from the requirement to heed the boundary between science and pseudoscience, from the need to offer genuine evidence for our versions of history, from scholars who point out that we have our facts wrong. In Foucault's account,

> Truth is a thing of this world: it is produced only by virtue of multiple forms of constraint. And it includes regular effects of power. Each society has its regime of truth, its 'general politics' of truth: that is, the types of discourse which it accepts and makes function as true …[8]

But the idea that this is emancipatory is a delusion. Take away reasoned argument and the requirement of reference to evidence – by discrediting them via deconstruction and rhetoric, via scare-quotes and mocking capital letters (e.g. Rorty's 'Way the World Is')[9] – and what *can* be left other than force of one kind or another? Either rhetorical force, via equivocation, fuzzy emotive vocabulary, straw men, exaggeration, appeals to the community or the nation or the people or the deity; or physical force, via laws and police. If the postmodernist academic Left is busy asserting that reason is merely a mask for power then who is going to prevent US legislators from simply mandating the teaching of ID or creationism in the secular public schools? And how will they go about it? With rhetoric and emotive appeals? But the other side, the theist side, is at least as good at that, and often better: evangelists tend to be good rhetoricians. Thus if postmodernism has busily eroded public belief in reason, evidence, logic and argument for the past 40 years or so, as it has, then all too often it is the case that rhetoric *is* all that's in play. And behold, it wins, even though the other side has the better case. All rhetoric has to do to win is convince people, it doesn't have to do it legitimately or reasonably or honestly.

Needless to say, this does happen, and not seldom. It's not a mere hypothetical or distant possibility, it's ongoing current reality. Postmodernist epistemic relativism itself relies heavily on rhetoric, as we've seen, and it enables rhetoric in others. So epistemic relativism makes possible a world where bad arguments and no evidence are helped to win public discussions over justified arguments and good evidence. This is emancipatory? Not in our view. It is not emancipatory because it helps emotive rhetoric to prevail over reason and evidence, which means it helps falsehood to prevail over truth. Being trapped in a world where lies can't be countered seems a strange idea of emancipation.

Alarmingly, some postmodernists don't stop with mere rhetoric but make actual programmatic statements about the status of evidence, point of view, trust, credibility and testimony, that if taken seriously would amount to a sort of How-to Guide for kangaroo courts. Consider, for instance, this comment by Thomas Gregor and Daniel Gross, on a statement from the American Anthropological Association report on *Darkness in El Dorado* which we discussed in Chapter 7:

> Consistent with not conducting an investigation, the task force asserts that neither *'did we consider the materials that we developed to be "evidence"* [rather] we present the various points of view that our interlocutors shared with us as important in their own right, as worthy of attention and reflection, *but not as "evidence" revealing that some event did or did not occur'* (AAA 2002a:9, emphasis added). This perspective reflects a philosophical stance of postmodern scholarship, in which objective truth may be seen as unattainable and contingent.[10]

A case of heads I win tails you lose, surely. The AAA declares that the 'points of view' their interlocutors (not witnesses, of course) shared with them are important and worthy of attention and reflection, but are not evidence revealing that 'some event' did or did not occur, just as the AAA declared that they were not conducting an investigation, but rather an enquiry. In the real world, however, that was a distinction without a difference: the enquiry with its interlocutors and points of view was able to damage Chagnon's reputation quite thoroughly enough. If postmodernism amounts to a thoroughgoing doubt that 'evidence' is possible or attainable, along with doubt-free respect and attention for points of view, then what is to prevent extrajudicial but destructive and punitive show trials from being staged whenever anyone has a grievance, no matter how ill-founded? Or for that matter, even *judicial* show trials. Too much attention to 'points of view' with too little scepticism can get innocent people convicted of crimes, on the basis of testimony from people with points of view but no evidence. A number of US court cases dealing with putative recovered memory, Satanic ritual abuse and child abuse in day-care facilities have achieved just such a result in the past two decades: law-enforcement officials and juries were solemnly instructed to 'listen to the children', and long prison sentences were handed out to people who were not, in fact, Satanists or secret child-murderers. The dangers seem obvious, but not everyone sees them. A reporter for the *Washington Post* made this observation in an article on the opening of the Smithsonian's new National Museum of the American Indian in September 2004:

> Once any outsider starts thinking like an anthropologist, it's hard not to start asking those bullying Margaret Mead questions. How do you know the natives are telling the truth? Is something sacred just because they say it's sacred? How do you know that they're not snowing you with all that talk of the Creator and the power of place and all the happy animism that runs through the general discourse of native life? If you believe that only native voices can get at the truth of native people, you must take it all in at face value. Truth is what individual people say about themselves,

beyond refute and suspicion – which is perhaps the most powerful, and radical, challenge that Postmodern thought has proposed.[11]

'Truth is what individual people say about themselves, beyond refute and suspicion' – that is certainly a powerful and radical challenge, but it is also more dangerous than it is emancipatory.

Eric Hobsbawm talks about related dangers in the first essay in his book *On History*. He points out that 'history is the raw material for national or ethnic or fundamentalist ideologies', that the past 'is perhaps the essential element in these ideologies' since '[t]he past legitimises'. Indian historian Romila Thapar makes the same point:

> Indian history from the perspective of the Hindutva ideology reintroduces ideas that have long been discarded and are of little relevance to an understanding of the past ... The rewriting of history according to these ideas is not to illumine the past but to allow an easier legitimation from the past for the political requirements of the present. The Hindutva obsession with identity is not a problem related to the early history of India but arises out of an attempt to manipulate identities in contemporary politics. Yet ironically, this can only be done if the existing interpretations of history are revised and forced into the Hindutva ideological mould.[12]

Hobsbawm used to think, he says, that the profession of history 'could at least do no harm' but now he knows it can: historians' studies can turn into bomb factories. Thus historians have 'a responsibility to historical facts in general' and to criticize the 'politico-ideological abuse of history in particular'. He is obliged to talk about this responsibility partly because of 'the rise of "postmodernist" intellectual fashions in Western universities which imply that "there is no clear difference between fact and fiction."'

> But there is, and for historians, even for the most militantly anti-positivist ones among us, the ability to distinguish between the two is absolutely fundamental. We cannot invent our facts ... Either the present Turkish government, which denies the attempted genocide of the Armenians in 1915, is right or it is not.

He cites the destruction of the Aodhya mosque by Hindu zealots on the supposed grounds that the Muslim conqueror Babur had built the mosque in a place sacred as the birthplace of Rama. 'My colleagues and friends in the Indian universities published a study showing (a) that nobody until the nineteenth century had suggested that Aodhya was the birthplace of Rama and (b) that the mosque was almost certainly not built in the time of Babur.' He adds that it hadn't had much effect on the rise of the Hindu party, 'but at least they did their duty as historians, for the benefit of those who can read and are exposed to the propaganda of intolerance ...'

He discusses the battle of Kosovo, Macedonia – and textbooks.

> These and many other attempts to replace history by myth and invention are not merely bad intellectual jokes. After all, they can determine what goes into schoolbooks, as the Japanese authorities knew, when they insisted on a sanitised version of the Japanese war in China for use in Japanese classrooms.[13]

Indeed. And as we write this, there are protests in Beijing and Guangzhou against precisely such sanitized versions of the Japanese war in China.

> Anti-Japanese protests have erupted in China for the second day running, spreading from Beijing to the southern province of Guangdong ... The protests were sparked by new Japanese schoolbooks, which many Chinese say whitewash Japan's occupation of much of China during the 1930s and early 1940s. Critics are angered that one of the books refers to the killing of more than 250,000 civilians by Japanese troops in the Chinese city of Nanjing in 1937 as an 'incident', rather than the 'massacre' it is known as elsewhere. They also say it glosses over mass sex slavery of Asian women by Japanese troops.[14]

The only way to counter historical lies, distortions, misrepresentations and disguises is with better accounts: better because more truthful. There is certainly no guarantee that the truth of the matter will be what one wants to hear, but the only alternative to trying to get at the truth is simply allowing exculpatory fictions to flourish. That outcome tends to outrage the many victims of historical atrocities. The survivors of Rwanda, Cambodia, Nanjing, South Africa, Chile, the Holocaust, the slave South, Armenia, and countless other 'incidents', want the truth on record. There is a reason truth and reconciliation commissions are called *truth* and reconciliation commissions. The truth is prior, and is a condition of the reconciliation; if the truth is not on offer, then reconciliation is not possible. If rhetoric is allowed to edge truth and truth-seeking out of the way, it will become difficult to get the truth on the record.

But the idea is abroad – partly due to that 'rise of postmodernist fashions' in universities – that in fact anti-realism, general scepticism (except about one's own truth-claims), anti-'scientism' are indeed emancipatory; that the power of science, rational enquiry, logic and evidence to get at the truth is a kind of tyranny, and something we need liberation from. But the real tyranny is being required to let humans – the community, the mullahs, the Vatican, the Southern Baptist Convention – decide what the truth is *independent* of the evidence – cut free from facts about the world. That's tyranny for you.

The 'postmodernist theologian' Philip Blond said on BBC Radio 3's *Nightwaves*:

> Science is wrong in our culture or has become unhinged in it seems to me two ways. First of all in contemporary culture science has converted its harmonic with truth into an absolutism, into a kind of quasi-fundamentalism, such that it claims to be the sole exhaustive universal model of truth. Secondly, in doing so, it has drained all other accounts, all broader or richer accounts of truth of any value. The absolutisation of science has resulted in the relativisation of morality, ethics, aesthetics, anything else you'd care to name.[15]

Because it was a radio discussion, with a moderator who chose which panellist spoke when, there was no opening for anyone to press him on what he meant and why he thought so – the statement went essentially unchallenged. Thus no one had an opportunity to point out that 'science' does no such thing (as claim to be the sole exhaustive model of truth), or to ask how, why, according to whom, it has 'drained' all other accounts of any value, and why, if that's true, other accounts are still so robust. The straw man was left quite unmolested. Blond's is a fairly typical example of anti-science rhetoric, which is why it is interesting: the rhetorical quality of the rhetoric is interesting. (One of the other participants, Norman Levitt, did later accuse Blond of using scare tactics.) It's the rhetoric of fear, of phobia. Rhetoric of fear replaces facts, and evidence of facts, with intensity. It bypasses the need to adduce evidence that the danger is real with alarm at how very scary it is. The alarm does the work of convincing, in defiance of the fact that if it's not happening or going to happen, its degree of scariness is pretty much irrelevant (except for story-telling purposes).

Is there anything very emancipatory about this sort of blind alley? Where we confuse the scariness of suggested dangers with the likelihood of their reality? Where alarmist jeremiads of this sort rely on brazen mischaracterizations of science that go uncorrected? Not in our view. Epicurus and Lucretius thought of their project as emancipatory: liberating the Hellenistic Greeks and the Romans from irrational, unnecessary fears of gods that either didn't exist or didn't meddle with humans, and death that no one experiences because the dead don't experience anything. The postmodernist project all too often seems rooted in an opposite impulse: not to liberate people from unnecessary illusory fears, but to generate new ones, and having generated them, magnify and entrench them. To tell spooky stories about power, regimes, authority, status, elites, expertise, that can sound bizarrely like paranoiac ravings about Freemasons and Illuminati. To tell heart-rending stories about disenchantment, alienation, reductionism, materialism, and the murder of spirituality, poetry, meaning, wonder, that make one feel as if attending the death of Tinkerbell. Fears created and magnified rather than debunked and dissipated. Is that emancipatory?

Of course, if the fears are justified, because the dangers are real – and especially if the dangers are real but deeply hidden, unperceived, denied – then it *is* ultimately emancipatory to point them out and try to do something about them. But the dangers in question are largely bogeymen dangers, straw men, fantasies: the kind of dangers that sadistic older siblings invent to torment younger ones.

And that's the trouble. Even leaving aside the fear aspect, and with it the question whether it is more emancipatory to dispel fears or to point out real but unperceived dangers – rhetoric itself in the absence of evidence is not emancipatory; rhetoric not as a communication aid, an addition to reliable evidence and sound inference, but as a substitute in their absence, is the very opposite of emancipatory. It's the equivalent of forced confessions – the kind that are thrown out of properly conducted courts, because they are not reliable.

Rhetoric is not emancipatory because it represents the replacement of truth by will. It is a Rube Goldberg contraption: a feeble contrivance of duct-tape and paper clips linking is to ought. But truth and will are two entirely different kinds of thing; will can do a lot, but it cannot determine what the truth is. A world in which people decide (wilfully) to pretend that it can, may be a lot of things – unified, reassuring, simplified – but emancipated is surely not one of them. That world is the Vatican's dream-world, where the pope declares what is true about anything he is moved to declare on, and his subjects accept that without further investigation. Mind-forg'd manacles, in short.

In the end, this boils down to preferences. Even the preference for a world where the lies of genocidal tyrannies are eventually corrected is still ultimately a preference. A highly reasonable, well-grounded preference, but still a preference. If we didn't have minds and emotions, and the moral thoughts that go with them, mass slaughters would just be something that happened, like rain.

Some people do prefer to live in a thought-world where priests and mullahs claim to decide what is true. Others prefer to live in a thought-world where ideas about what is true are lenient, flexible, fuzzy around the edges; where it is possible to sort-of-believe, half-believe and half-hope, believe in an as if or storytelling or daydreaming way. Others prefer – genuinely prefer, not merely think they're supposed to – to try to figure out what really is true, as opposed to what might be, or appears to be, or should be. This is a preference. One can adduce moral and psychological reasons for both preferences. The reasons we've given for thinking truth matters rest on preferences, and there's no final definitive knock-down case for them, at least not that we've been able to think up or find. But reasons can be good reasons without being final ones.

And one last good reason for thinking that truth matters, it seems to us, is all about preferences, in the largest and most humanly important sense. It's about happiness, flourishing, enthusiasm, about what makes life worth living, why we prefer being awake to being asleep, why it's a privilege to be human. It's about why truth *matters*. Really matters. Not in a dull perfunctory dutiful sense, but in a real, lived, felt sense – 'on the pulses', as Keats put it.

This is the kind of mattering we're talking about here – personal but also public, subjective but also communicable and sharable, immediate but also permanent, cognitive but also emotional. In a way it's just as much about community and solidarity as Rorty's vision is, but it's a community that thinks truth matters rather than one that prefers solidarity to truth. Truth is perhaps the capital city on that mattering map.

This reason is based on the thought that enquiry, curiosity, interest, investigation, explanation-seeking, are hugely important components of human happiness. This doesn't seem to be a terribly popular thought right now. Public rhetoric tends to aim much lower, for some reason. It seems to see us all as hunkered down, and settling. Settling for minimal, parochial, almost biological satisfactions – family, safety, money. But that underestimates us. We want more than that. We want to ask questions, we want to learn, we want to understand. That's a very human taste and pleasure. Again, as we said in Chapter 1, it seems a waste not to use human capacities and abilities. Anyone can settle for just survival and reproduction and comfort, but we can do more. That's a privilege – and it seems a kind of sacrilege not to use it.

And real enquiry presupposes that truth matters. That it is true that there is a truth of the matter we're investigating, even if it turns out that we can't find it. Maybe the next generation can, or two or three or ten after that, or maybe just someone more skilled than we are. But we have to think there is something to find in order for enquiry to be genuine enquiry and not just an arbitrary game that doesn't go anywhere. We like games, but we also like genuine enquiry. *That's* why truth matters.

Postmodern (and postmodern-aided traditional) attacks on science and truth of the sort quoted above tend to frame science and enquiry as impoverished in various ways: arid, cold, unfeeling, mechanical, dull, empty of poetry and colour and life, devoid of wonder. This is an old Romantic trope – Blake's 'single vision and Newton's sleep', Keats's 'cold philosophy would clip an angel's wings', Wordsworth's 'they murder to dissect'. But scientists with real experience of enquiry and discovery think that Blake, Keats and Wordsworth were simply wrong, and that so are their contemporary avatars. Richard Dawkins for example:

> To accuse science of robbing life of the warmth that makes it worth living is so preposterously mistaken, so diametrically opposed to my own feelings and those of most working scientists, I am almost driven to the despair of which I am wrongly suspected … The feeling of awed wonder that science can give us is one of the highest experiences of which the human psyche is capable. It is a deep aesthetic passion to rank with the finest that music and poetry can deliver.[16]

And Matt Ridley:

> The one thing I would try to teach the world about science is *that science is not a catalogue of facts, but a search for new mysteries.* Science increases the store of wonder and mystery in the world; it does not erode it.
>
> The myth, started by the Romantic poets, that science gets rid of mysteries was well nailed by Albert Einstein – whose thought experiments

about relativity are far more otherworldly, elusive, thrilling and baffling than anything dreamt up by poets. Isaac Newton showed us the mysteries of deep space, Charles Darwin showed us the mysteries of deep time, and Francis Crick and James D. Watson showed us the mysteries of deep encoding. To get rid of those insights would be to reduce the world's stock of awe.[17]

That's why truth matters.

Notes

Chapter 1

1. Hidden god.
2. Jamie Whyte, *Crimes Against Logic* (New York: McGraw Hill, 2005), pp. 9–10.
3. Salman Rushdie, 'Defend the right to be offended', *Open Democracy* (2 July 2005).
4. Being pedants, we feel compelled to note that freedom of thought doesn't actually become *impossible* in such a situation, though it does become more difficult and inhibited. Thought is always constrained and shaped by innumerable cultural and social influences, so the matter is not one of complete freedom versus complete suppression.
5. In a sense it weakens its own case by doing so – at least, for those given to critical thinking – but in another sense it doesn't, because the sad truth is that the Taboo move very often does work. Declare yourself outraged and offended, and people do shut up, or at least hold meetings and conciliation discussions.
6. Voltaire, *Philosophical Dictionary*, trans. Theodore Besterman (London: Penguin, 1972), p. 49.
7. Ophelia Benson, 'An interview with Rebecca Goldstein', *Butterflies and Wheels*, http://www.butterfliesandwheels.com/articleprint.php?-num=116 (accessed 16 July 2005).
8. Claudia Roth Pierpont, 'The measure of America', *The New Yorker* (8 March 2004): 55.
9. Ibid.

10. Derek Freeman, *Margaret Mead and the Heretic* (London: Penguin, 1983 and 1996), p. 282.

11. Edmund Gosse, *Father and Son*, Ch. 5, Project Gutenberg. http://www.gutenberg.org/etext/2540 (accessed 15 May 2005).

12. Richard Evans, *In Defense of History* (New York: Norton, 1999), pp. 106–7.

13. Richard Evans, contribution to the 'Great Debate on History and Postmodernism' (University of Sydney, 27 July 2002), published as 'Postmodernism and history', *Butterflies and Wheels*, http://www.butterfliesandwheels.com/articleprint.php?num=5 (accessed 15 May 2005).

Chapter 2

1. Herodotus, *The History*, trans. George C. Macaulay, http://www.gutenberg.org/etext/2707 (accessed 20 May 2005).

2. Herodotus, *The History*, 1.135, trans. David Grene (Chicago, IL: University of Chicago Press, 1987), p. 97.

3. Ibid., 4.76: 308.

4. Michel de Montaigne, *The Complete Essays*, 1.31, trans. and ed. M.A. Screech (London: Penguin, 1991), p. 231.

5. Richard H. Popkin, *The History of Scepticism* (Berkeley, CA: University of California Press, 1979), p. xiii.

6. Ibid., p. 1.

7. Ibid., p. 3.

8. Richard H. Popkin and Avrum Stoll, *Skeptical Philosophy for Everyone* (Amherst, NY: Prometheus Books, 2002), p. 55.

9. Popkin, *Scepticism*, p. 55.

10. René Descartes, *Descartes' Discourse on Method, and Other Writings*, trans. Arthur Wollaston (London: Penguin, 1960), pp. 38–9.

11. Ibid., p. 102.

12. Ibid., p. 108.

13. For a discussion of some of them, see Simon Blackburn, *Truth: A Guide for the Perplexed* (London: Penguin, 2005), Ch. 6.

14. The first chapter of McGinn's book *The Mysterious Flame* has a section on 'conscious meat'. The section was inspired by the science fiction writer Terry Bisson.

15. Cited in Jeremy Stangroom, *What Scientists Think* (London: Routledge, 2005), pp. 84–5.

16. John Gray makes a more sophisticated version of this kind of argument in his book *Straw Dogs*.

17. David Stove, '"I only am escaped alone to tell thee:" epistemology and the Ishmael effect', in *The Plato Cult* (Oxford: Blackwell, 1991), pp. 61–82. It's called the 'Ishmael effect', after the narrator of Melville's *Moby Dick*, who claimed to have been the lone survivor of an unfortunate incident with a whale, but he cannot possibly have been, given the truth of his story.

18. Blackburn, *Truth*, p. 48. Blackburn discusses the 'Ishmael effect' as it relates to relativist and sceptical arguments. See Ch. 3 of *Truth*.

19. Cited in Maria Baghramian, *Relativism* (London: Routledge, 2004), p. 67.

20. Ted Kinnaman points out that this argument involves a nice play on the German word 'Glaube', which can mean both 'belief' and 'faith'. See http://www.iep.utm.edu/h/Hamann.htm (accessed 17 May 2005).

21. Frederick Beiser, 'Johann Georg Hamann', *Routledge Encyclopedia of Philosophy* (London: Routledge, 1998).

22. Baghramian, *Relativism*, p. 67.

23. For a satirical treatment of this tendency, see Ophelia Benson and Jeremy Stangroom, 'Anticipate', *The Dictionary of Fashionable Nonsense* (London: Souvenir Press 2004), p. 10.

24. The similarity exists only at one level; Hamann also had the view that language is divinely inspired.

25. Ludwig Wittgenstein, *Philosophical Investigations*, 3rd edn (Oxford: Blackwell, 1967), p. 47.

26. Ibid., p. 20.

27. The caveat here is that there are about as many interpretations of precisely what Wittgenstein meant by 'forms of life' as there are Wittgenstein scholars.

28. A. C. Grayling, *Wittgenstein: A Very Short Introduction* (Oxford: Oxford University Press, 2001), p. 97.

29. Ibid.

30. Wittgenstein, *Philosophical Investigations*, p. 226.

31. Thomas Kuhn, *The Structure of Scientific Revolutions*, 3rd edn (Chicago, IL: University of Chicago Press, 1996), pp. 16–17.

32. George Ritzer, 'Sociology: a multiple paradigm science', *The American Sociologist*, 10.3 (August 1975): 157.

33. Kuhn, *Scientific Revolutions*, p. 150.

34. Baghramian, *Relativism*, p. 187.

35. Cited in Susan Haack, *Defending Science – Within Reason* (Amherst, NY: Prometheus Books, 2003), p. 33.

36. Kuhn, *Scientific Revolutions*, p. 206.

37. John Horgan, *The End of Science* (New York: Broadway Books, 1997), p. 122.

38. Thomas Kuhn, Rothschild Lecture, 1992, cited at http://www.butter-fliesandwheels.com/quoteprint.php?author=Thomas%20Kuhn&type=w (accessed 18 July 2005).

39. Cited in Morris Dickstein, *The Revival of Pragmatism* (Durham, NC: Duke University Press, 1988), p. 11.

40. The point here, of course, is not these particular beliefs; the Azande, for example, will possibly believe none of these things. But rather that for any culture there are these kinds of beliefs (i.e., things which are taken to be true in a more than provisional, possibly true sense).

41. Interesting in this regard is that Norman Levitt, the author of *Higher Superstition: The Academic Left and its Quarrels with Science*, has said that he first became interested in the various kinds of truth-denial after his daughter became sick with an illness which twenty years earlier would have been fatal, thereby bringing it home to him just how much is at stake with this stuff.

Chapter 3

1. Morris Dickstein, Introduction, *The Revival of Pragmatism* (Durham, NC: Duke University Press, 1998), p. 11. See also John Patrick Diggins, *The Promise of Pragmatism* (Chicago, IL: University of Chicago Press, 1994).

2. It also, at least in the USA, encouraged the turning away from bread-and-butter issues and the working class, since working-class opposition to the war, though widespread, was not universal, and a myth arose that the working class as a whole was flag-wavingly pro-war.

3. Sandra Harding, *Whose Science? Whose Knowledge?* (Ithaca, NY: Cornell University Press, 1991), pp. 106–15.

4. Ibid., p. 48.
5. Ibid., p. 47.
6. Ibid., pp. 51–2.
7. Nancy Hartsock, 'The feminist standpoint', cited in Harding, *Whose Science?*, p. 131.
8. Alan Sokal and Jean Bricmont, *Intellectual Impostures* (Amherst, NY: Profile Books, 1998, 2003), p. 85.
9. Bruno Latour, *Pandora's Hope* (Cambridge, MA: Harvard University Press, 1999), p. 310.
10. Ibid., p. 296.
11. Ibid., p. 149.
12. See ibid., p. 158.
13. Ibid., p. 159.
14. Ibid., p. 154.
15. Ibid., p. 117.
16. Ibid., p. 118.
17. Ibid., p. 120.
18. Ibid., p. 122.
19. Cited in Sokal and Bricmont, *Intellectual Impostures*, p. 85.
20. Ibid.
21. Latour, *Pandora's Hope*, p. 128.
22. Cited ibid., p. 129 (our italics).
23. Andrew Ross, *Strange Weather* (London: Verso, 1991), p. 1.
24. Ibid., p. 11.
25. Ibid., p. 12.
26. Ibid., p. 11.
27. Ibid., p. 39.
28. Ibid., p. 42.
29. Ibid., p. 113.
30. Andrew Ross, 'Reflections on the Sokal affair', in *The Sokal Hoax* (Lincoln, NB: University of Nebraska Press, 2000), p. 245.
31. Ibid., p. 60.

Chapter 4

1. David Bloor, *Knowledge and Social Imagery* (Chicago, IL: University of Chicago Press, 1991), p. 3.
2. Ibid., p. 46.
3. James Robert Brown, *Who Rules in Science?* (Cambridge, MA: Harvard University Press, 2001), pp. 118–19.
4. After Philip Kitcher, 'A plea for science studies', in Noretta Koertge (ed.), *A House Built on Sand* (Oxford: Oxford University Press, 1998), pp. 34–5.
5. Ibid., p. 36.
6. Susan Haack, *Defending Science – Within Reason* (Amherst, NY: Prometheus Books, 2003), p. 180.
7. James Robert Brown, *Who Rules in Science?*, p. 158.
8. Kitcher, 'A plea for science studies', p. 39.
9. Martin J. S. Rudwick, *The Great Devonian Controversy* (Chicago, IL: University of Chicago Press, 1985), p. 15.
10. Ibid.
11. Ibid., p. 6.
12. Ibid.
13. Kitcher, 'A plea for science studies', p. 44.
14. Ibid., p. 55.

Chapter 5

1. For a modern treatment of this phenomenon, see Nils Roll-Hansen, *The Lysenko Effect* (Amherst, NY: Humanity Books, 2005).
2. Cited in *The Rise and Fall of T.D. Lysenko*, trans. I. Michael Lerner (New York: Columbia University Press, 1969), Zhores A. Medvedev, p. 107.
3. Herbert Spencer, *Social Statics*, http://oll.libertyfund.org/Texts/LFBooks/Spencer0236/SocialStatics/0331_Bk.html (accessed 25 May 2005).
4. Herbert Spencer, *Study of Sociology*, http://oll.libertyfund.org/Home3/Book.php?recordID=0623 (accessed 24 May 2005).
5. Charles Darwin, *The Descent of Man*, http://www.infidels.org/library/historical/charles_darwin/descent_of_man/chapter_05.html (accessed 25 May 2005).

6. Francis Galton, 'Eugenics: its definition, scope and aims', *American Journal of Sociology* 10.1 (1904).

7. Ibid.

8. Ibid.

9. Caleb Williams Saleeby, 'The obstacles to eugenics', *Sociological Review* 2 (n.d.): 236.

10. *The Passing of the Great Race* was influential as well as popular, partly because it included a preface by Henry Fairfield Osborn, the curator of palaeontology and president of the board of the American Museum of Natural History.

11. Internet source, now obsolete.

12. 'Find law for legal professionals', n. 4, http://caselaw.lp.findlaw.com/scripts/getcase.pl?court=US&vol=388&invol=1 (accessed 15 May 2005).

13. It should be noted that there is some debate about this figure. Many of these people signed a consent form. However, even in these cases, there is good reason to suppose that there had been a significant amount of coercion.

14. The Catholic Church had consistently maintained its opposition to eugenics.

15. Franz Boas, *Race and Democratic Society* (New York: Biblio and Tannen, 1969), pp. 18–19.

16. See Carl N. Degler, *In Search of Human Nature: The Decline and Revival of Darwinism in American Social Thought* (Oxford: Oxford University Press, 1991), p. 209.

17. Ibid., pp. 209–10.

18. See ibid., pp. 187–211.

19. Edward Larson says in his 1997 book on the Scopes trial, *Summer for the Gods*: 'As a devout believer in peace, Bryan could scarcely understand how supposedly Christian nations could engage in such a brutal war until two scholarly books attributed it to misguided Darwinian thinking', citing *Headquarters Nights*, by Stanford zoologist Vernon Kellogg, and *The Science of Power* by sociologist Benjamin Kidd. (Edward J. Larson, *Summer for the Gods: The Scopes Trial and America's Continuing Debate Over Science and Religion* [Cambridge, MA: Harvard University Press, 1997], p. 40.).

20. Stephen Jay Gould, *Bully for Brontosaurus: Reflections in Natural History* (New York: Norton, 1992), p. 428.

21. Ibid., p. 429.

22. Richard Dawkins, *The Selfish Gene*, 2nd edn (Oxford: Oxford University Press, 1989), p. v.

23. Mary Midgley, 'Gene juggling', *Philosophy* 54.210 (1979): 439–40.

24. Dawkins, *The Selfish Gene*, p. 4.

25. Midgley, 'Gene juggling', p. 439.

26. Andrew Brown, *The Darwin Wars* (New York: Simon & Schuster, 1999), p. 92.

27. Mary Midgley, 'Selfish genes and social Darwinism', *Philosophy* 58.225 (July 1983): 365.

28. Dawkins, *The Selfish Gene*, pp. 2–3.

29. Richard Dawkins, *A Devil's Chaplain*, ed. Latha Menon (London: Weidenfeld & Nicolson, 2003), p. 8.

30. Ibid., pp. 9–11.

31. Richard Dawkins, *The Extended Phenotype* (Oxford: Oxford University Press, 1982), p. 13.

32. Ibid.

33. Richard Dawkins, 'In defence of selfish genes', *Philosophy* 56.218, (October 1981): 558.

34. Midgley herself makes this kind of point in 'Selfish genes' (pp. 366–7).

35. Midgley, 'Gene-juggling', p. 449.

36. Midgley, 'Selfish genes', p. 369.

37. Steven Rose, Leon J. Kamin and Richard Lewontin, *Not in Our Genes* (London: Penguin, 1991), p. 31.

38. Ibid., p. 30.

39. *Red Pepper* (September 1997): 23.

40. Cited in Jeremy Stangroom, *What Scientists Think* (London: Routledge, 2005), p. 167.

41. *Guardian*, 13 October 2004.

42. Dawkins, *The Selfish Gene*, p. 268.

43. Cited in Julian Baggini and Jeremy Stangroom, *What Philosophers Think* (London: Continuum, 2003), pp. 47–8.

Chapter 6

1. Stuart Hall and Martin Jacques, 'People aid: a new politics sweeps the land', *Marxism Today* (July 1986).

2. Stuart Hall and Martin Jacques, 'No light at the end of the tunnel', *Marxism Today* (December 1986).

3. Madeleine Bunting, 'We are the people', *Guardian* (17 February 2003).

4. Hannah Arendt, 'Lying in politics', *Crises of the Republic* (New York: Harcourt Brace, 1972), p. 5.

5. Steven Pinker's *The Blank Slate* is a book-length exposition of this point.

6. Friedrich Engels, in Karl Marx and Friedrich Engels, *Basic Writings on Politics and Philosophy*, ed. Lewis S. Feuer (London: Collins/Fontana, 1981), pp. 146–7.

7. Cited in Jeremy Stangroom, *What Scientists Think* (London: Routledge, 2005), p. 34.

8. Friedrich Engels, *The Origins of the Family, Private Property and the State*, http://www.marxists.org/archive/marx/works/1884/origin-family/ch02d.htm (accessed 24 May 2005).

9. Ibid.

10. Cited in Julian Baggini and Jeremy Stangroom, *What Philosophers Think* (London: Continuum, 2003), p. 35.

11. John Stuart Mill, *The Subjection of Women*, Ch. 1, http://www.constitution.org/jsm/women.htm (accessed 24 May 2005).

12. Sandra Harding, *Whose Science? Whose Knowledge?* (Ithaca, NY: Cornell University Press, 1991), p. 150.

13. Margaret Talbot, 'Teen Angels', the *New Republic* (22 July 2002), http://www.newamerica.net/index.cfm?pg=article&DocID=908 (accessed 21 May 2005).

14. Mary Field Belenky, Blythe McVicker Clinchy, Nancy Rule Goldberger and Jill Mattuck Tarule, *Women's Ways of Knowing: The Development of Self, Voice and Mind* (New York: Basic Books, 1986).

15. Susan Haack, *Manifesto of a Passionate Moderate* (Chicago, IL: University of Chicago Press, 1998), p. 125.

16. Daphne Patai and Noretta Koertge, *Professing Feminism* (New York: Basic Books, 1994), p. 167.

17. Janet Radcliffe Richards, 'Why Feminist Epistemology Isn't', *The Flight From Science and Reason*, ed. Paul R. Gross, Norman Levitt and Martin Lewis (New York: New York Academy of Sciences, 1997), p. 407.

18. John McWhorter, *Authentically Black* (New York: Gotham Books, 2003), p. 180.

19. Ortiz de Montellano, http://www.csicop.org/si/9111/minority.html part

one http://www.csicop.org/si/9201/minority.html part two (accessed 21 May 2005).

20. Ortiz de Montellano, 'Afrocentric pseudoscience: the miseducation of African Americans', *The Flight From Science and Reason*, p. 561.

21. Ibid.

22. *Skeptical Inquirer*, (Autumn 1991).

23. Mary Lefkowitz, 'The ancient world as seen by Afrocentrists', *Butterflies and Wheels*, http://www.butterfliesandwheels.com/articleprint.php?-num=3 (accessed 24 May 2005).

24. Mary Lefkowitz, *Not out of Africa* (New York: Basic Books, 1996), p. xv.

25. Ibid., p. xi.

26. Ibid., p. xii.

27. Ibid., pp. 1–2.

28. Ibid., p. 2.

29. Ibid., p. 4.

30. Ibid., pp. xiii–xiv.

31. Cited in Jeremy Stangroom, *What Scientists Think*, p. 143.

32. Richard Evans, 'Postmodernism and history', contribution to the 'Great Debate on History and Postmodernism', University of Sydney, Australia, 27 July 2002. *Butterflies and Wheels*, http://www.butterfliesandwheels.-com/articleprint.php?num=5 (accessed 24 May 2005).

33. Meera Nanda, *Prophets Facing Backward* (New Brunswick and London: Rutgers University Press, 2003), p. xi.

34. Ibid., p. 2.

35. Barbara Forrest and Paul R. Gross, *Creationism's Trojan Horse* (Oxford: Oxford University Press, 2004).

36. Latha Menon, 'Saffron infusion: Hindutva, history, and education', *Butterflies and Wheels*, http://www.butterfliesandwheels.com/article-print.php?num=48 (accessed 24 May 2005).

37. Nanda, *Prophets Facing Backward*, *passim*.

38. http://www.cr.nps.gov/aad/kennewick/ (accessed 21 May 2005).

39. Andrew L. Slayman, 'A battle over bones', *Archaeology* 50.1, http://www.archaeology.org/9701/etc/specialreport.html (accessed 21 May 2005).

40. BBC News, 21 July 2004, http://news.bbc.co.uk/2/hi/science/nature/3909421.stm (accessed 21 May 2005).

41. Friends of America's Past, Public Comment to the NAGPRA Review Committee, 31 May 2001, http://www.friendsofpast.org/nagpra/comment-02.html (accessed 21 May 2005).

42. Armand Minthorn, 'Human remains should be reburied', http://www.umatilla.nsn.us/kman1.html (accessed 21 May 2005).

43. Nanda, *Prophets Facing Backward*, p. xii.

Chapter 7

1. See www.pmdocs.com (accessed 21 May 2005).

2. http://www.ash.org.uk/html/conduct/pdfs/2063791193.pdf (accessed 21 May 2005).

3. http://www.ash.org.uk/html/conduct/pdfs/2500048956.pdf (accessed 21 May 2005).

4. See ibid.

5. This was disputed by the *Lancet*. See, for example, the *New Scientist* (23 May 1998): 16.

6. The *Lancet* (8 April 2000): 1253–9.

7. See ibid., p. 1254.

8. Ibid., p. 1258.

9. http://www.ash.org.uk/html/conduct/pdfs/2023012742.pdf (accessed 21 May 2005).

10. http://www.ash.org.uk/html/conduct/pdfs/2501474296.pdf (accessed 21 May 2005).

11. Deborah H. Barnes and Lisa A. Bero, 'Why review articles on the health effects of passive smoking reach different conclusions', *Journal of the American Medical Association* (20 May 1998): 1566–70.

12. Ibid., p. 1570.

13. See, for example, *New Scientist* (May 2003): 23.

14. See http://www.ucsusa.org/global_environment/rsi/page.cfm?pageID=1601 (accessed 21 May 2005).

15. Cited in Jeremy Stangroom, *What Scientists Think* (London: Routledge, 2005), p. 178.

16. Cited ibid., p. 146.

17. Brigham Young University mission statement, http://unicom.byu.edu/about/aims/printable.html?lms=8 (accessed 18 July 2005).

18. http://www.byu.edu/fc/pages/refmapages/acadfree.html (accessed 21 May 2005).

19. Brigham Young University mission statement.

20. See http://campuslife.byu.edu/honorcode/ (accessed 21 May 2005).

21. 'Academic freedom and tenure: Brigham Young University', *Academe* (September–October 1997): 52–71.

22. 'The issue of academic freedom: an interview with Jim Gordon', *Brigham Young Magazine* (Winter 1997).

23. Cited in 'Academic freedom and tenure', p. 52.

24. Ibid., p. 65.

25. Ibid., p. 70.

26. Ibid., p. 67.

27. http://www.columbia.edu/cu/news/05/03/ad_hoc_grievance_committee_report.html (accessed 21 May 2005).

28. Ibid.

29. Ibid.

30. Ibid.

31. Joseph Massad, Statement to the Ad Hoc Committee 1 (14 March 2005).

32. Charles Jacobs, 'Becoming Columbia', *Columbia Spectator* (11 April 2005).

33. See, for example, http://www.censoringthought.org/behindthemyth.html (accessed 21 May 2005).

34. See, for example, Scott Jaschik, 'War and Peace at Columbia', *Inside Higher Ed* (1 April 2005), http://www.insidehighered.com/news/2005/04/01/columbia (accessed 21 May 2005).

35. David Lehman, *Signs of the Times* (London: Andre Deutsch, 1991), p. 45.

36. See ibid., p. 43.

37. Ibid., p. 56.

38. Ibid., p. 55.

39. Ibid., p. 52.

40. Ibid.

41. William Kerrigan, 'The falls of academe', in Mark Edmundson (ed.), *Wild Orchids and Trotsky* (London: Penguin, 1993), p. 161.

42. Mark Crispin Miller, (London: 'Class dismissed') *CONTEXT*, 4, online edn, http://www.centerforbookculture.org/context/no4/miller.html (accessed 21 May 2005).

43. John Strausbaugh, 'Eggheads' naughty word games', *New York Times* (27 December 2004).

44. http://members.aol.com/archaeodog/darkness_in_el_dorado/documents/0090.htm (accessed 11 May 2005).

45. http://www.guardian.co.uk/Archive/Article/0,4273,4067128,00.html (accessed 11 May 2005).

46. See http://www.psych.ucsb.edu/research/cep/eldorado/lindee.html (accessed 11 May 2005).

47. 'ASHG commentary: response to allegations against James V. Neel in *Darkness in El Dorado*, by Patrick Tierney', *American Journal of Human Genetics* 70 (2002): 2.

48. http://www4.nas.edu/NAS/nashome.nsf/Multi+Database+Search/57065F16FF258371852569920052D283?OpenDocument (accessed 11 May 2005).

49. Cited in Peter Monaghan, 'Bitter warfare in anthropology', *Chronicle of Higher Education* (26 October 1994).

50. Cited in Michael D'Antonio, 'Napoleon Chagnon's war of discovery', *Los Angeles Times Magazine* (20 January 2000).

51. http://cogweb.ucla.edu/Debate/UMichOnChagnon.html (accessed 11 May 2005).

52. Thomas Gregor and Daniel R. Gross, 'Guilt by association: the culture of accusation and the American Anthropological Association's investigation of *Darkness in El Dorado*', *American Anthropologist* 106.4 (December 2004): 695–6.

53. Ibid., p. 688.

54. Ibid., p. 689.

55. Pauline Rosenau, cited ibid., p. 690.

56. Ibid.

57. See, for example, Leslie E. Sponsel and Thomas Gregor (eds), *The Anthropology of Peace and Nonviolence* (Boulder, CO: Rienner, 1994).

Chapter 8

1. Richard Rorty, *Contingency, Irony, Solidarity* (Cambridge: Cambridge University Press, 1989), pp. 51–2.
2. Michael Lynch, *True to Life: Why Truth Matters* (New York: MIT Press, 2004), p. 164.
3. Susan Haack, *Manifesto of a Passionate Moderate* (Chicago, IL: University of Chicago Press, 1998), p. 19.
4. Ibid., p. 67 n. 29.
5. http://www.nationalreview.com/comment/comment-goldblatt011603.asp (accessed 21 May 2005).
6. http://www.humanities.uci.edu/remembering_jd/ (accessed 21 May 2005).
7. http://www.humanities.uci.edu/remembering_jd/butler_judith.htm (accessed 21 May 2005).
8. Michel Foucault, 'Truth and power', *The Foucault Reader*, ed. P. Rabinow (New York: Pantheon, 1987), pp. 73–4.
9. Richard Rorty, *Philosophy and Social Hope* (London: Penguin, 1999), p. 33.
10. Thomas Gregor and Daniel R. Gross, 'Guilt by association: the culture of accusation and the American Anthropological Association's investigation of *Darkness in El Dorado*', *American Anthropologist* 106.4 (December 2004): 691.
11. Philip Kennicott, *Washington Post* (19 September 2004), http://www.washingtonpost.com/ac2/wp-dyn/A28890-2004Sep17?language=printer (accessed 23 May 2005).
12. Romila Thapar, 'Hindutva and history', *Frontline* 17.20 (October 2000), http://www.dalitstan.org/holocaust/negation/thaphist.html (accessed 21 May 2005).
13. Eric Hobsbawm, *On History* (New York: The New Press, 1997), pp. 5–7.
14. http://news.bbc.co.uk/2/hi/asia-pacific/4429809.stm (accessed 21 May 2005).
15. Philip Blond, *Nightwaves*, BBC Radio 3.
16. Richard Dawkins, *Unweaving the Rainbow* (New York: Houghton Mifflin, 1998), p. x.
17. *Spiked* science survey, 'If you could teach the world just one thing,' http://www.spiked-online.com/articles/0000000CAA95.htm (accessed 21 May 2005).

Index